MW01487640

Life After Leaving

WRITING LIVES
ETHNOGRAPHIC NARRATIVES

Series Editors:
Arthur P. Bochner & Carolyn Ellis
University of South Florida

Writing Lives: Ethnographic Narratives publishes narrative representations of qualitative research projects. The series editors seek manuscripts that blur the boundaries between humanities and social sciences. We encourage novel and evocative forms of expressing concrete lived experience, including autoethnographic, literary, poetic, artistic, visual, performative, critical, multi-voiced, conversational, and co-constructed representations. We are interested in ethnographic narratives that depict local stories; employ literary modes of scene setting, dialogue, character development, and unfolding action; and include the author's critical reflections on the research and writing process, such as research ethics, alternative modes of inquiry and representation, reflexivity, and evocative storytelling. Proposals and manuscripts should be directed to abochner@cas.usf.edu

Volumes in this series:

Erotic Mentoring: Women's Transformations in the University,
Janice Hocker Rushing

Intimate Colonialism: Head, Heart, and Body in West African Development Work, Laurie L. Charlés

Last Writes: A Daybook for a Dying Friend, Laurel Richardson

A Trickster in Tweed: The Quest for Quality in a Faculty Life,
Thomas F. Frentz

Guyana Diaries: Women's Lives Across Difference, Kimberly D. Nettles

Writing Qualitative Inquiry: Selves, Stories and Academic Life,
H. L. Goodall, Jr.

Accidental Ethnography: An Inquiry into Family Secrecy,
Christopher N. Poulos

Revision: Autoethnographic Reflections on Life and Work, Carolyn Ellis

Leaning: A Poetics of Personal Relationships, Ronald J. Pelias

Narrating the Closet: An Autoethnography of Same-Sex Attraction,
Tony E. Adams

Life After Leaving: The Remains of Spousal Abuse, Sophie Tamas

Life After Leaving
The Remains of Spousal Abuse

Sophie Tamas

Left Coast
Press Inc.

Walnut Creek, California

LEFT COAST PRESS, INC.
1630 North Main Street, #400
Walnut Creek, CA 94596
http://www.LCoastPress.com

Copyright © 2011 by Left Coast Press, Inc.

All rights reserved. No part of this publication may be reproduced, stored in a retrieval system, or transmitted in any form or by any means, electronic, mechanical, photocopying, recording, or otherwise, without the prior permission of the publisher.

ISBN 978-1-61132-061-9 hardcover
ISBN 978-1-61132-062-6 paperback
ISBN 978-1-61132-063-3 electronic

Library of Congress Cataloging-in-Publication Data

Tamas, Sophie.
  Life after leaving : the remains of spousal abuse / Sophie Tamas.
    p. cm. — (Writing lives : ethnographic narratives)
  Includes bibliographical references and index.
  ISBN 978-1-61132-061-9 (hbk. : alk. paper) — ISBN 978-1-61132-062-6 (pbk. : alk. paper) — ISBN 978-1-61132-063-3 (ebook)
  1. Tamas, Sophie. 2. Abused wives—Canada—Psychology. 3. Abused wives—Canada—Drama. 4. Abused wives—Rehabilitation. I. Title.
  HV6626.23.C2T36 2011
  362.82′92092—dc23
                        2011022308

Printed in the United States of America

∞™ The paper used in this publication meets the minimum requirements of American National Standard for Information Sciences—Permanence of Paper for Printed Library Materials, ANSI/NISO Z39.48–1992.

CONTENTS

International Institute for Qualitative Methodology

The International Institute for Qualitative Methodology (IIQM), under the auspices of the Faculty of Nursing at the University of Alberta, was founded in 1998 to facilitate the development of qualitative research methods across a wide variety of academic disciplines through research, publications, conferences, and workshops. The Institute sponsors volumes that have received the Dissertation Award of the Institute, then were revised for publication. This book is a revised version of the author's award-winning dissertation.

Other IIQM sponsored volumes available from Left Coast Press, Inc. at www.LCoastPress.com:

Irena Madjar, *Giving Comfort and Inflicting Pain*

Ian William Sewall, *The Folkloral Voice*

Karen Martin, *When a Baby Dies of SIDS: The Parents' Grief and Search for Reason*

Claudia Malacrida, *Mourning the Dreams: How Parents Create Meaning from Miscarriage, Stillbirth, and Early Infant Death*

Hedy Bach, *A Visual Narrative Concerning Curriculum, Girls, Photography, Etc.*

Rodney Evans, *The Pedagogic Principal*

Colleen Reid, *The Wounds of Exclusion: Poverty, Women's Health, and Social Justice*

Lynne Wiltse, *Cultural Diversity and Discourse Practices in Grade Nine*

Hazel K. Platzer, *Positioning Identities: Lesbians' and Gays' Experiences with Mental Health Care*

Helen Vallianatos, *Poor and Pregnant in New Delhi, India*

Linde Zingaro, *Speaking Out: Storytelling for Social Change*

Sheri Leafgren, *Reuben's Fall: A Rhizomatic Analysis of Disobedience in Kindergarten*

Kaela Jubas, *The Politics of Shopping: What Consumers Learn about Identity, Globalization and Social Change*

ACKNOWLEDGMENTS

I would like to thank, in no particular order, the people without whom this book would not exist:

◙ My dissertation supervisor, Dr. Sarah Todd. I met Sarah by knocking on her office door, nervously describing my proposed inquiry, and asking if she'd consider supervising it. I had little hope. I was not from her department, she was so well loved by her students that she probably would not have the time, and she was about to be going on maternity leave and sabbatical. But she said yes. When I am feeling bleak, I remember this as a moment of pure, astonishing grace, one of the great pivots of fortune in my life.

◙ My research participants. These women gave me the gift of their time and stories, and trusted me to do something useful with them. I will keep trying to do so.

◙ My parents, who always believed I was a writer and encouraged me, even if they worried about what I might write.

◙ My sweet girls—the three wonderful creatures who give structure and meaning to my life.

◙ Mitch and Carolyn—my publisher and editor—for their insightful critiques and unfailing support.

Finally, even though he finds dedications cloying, I would like to dedicate this book to Shawn.

I truly believe that
unless this work is personal,
you are not really doing it.

—*Teresa Bernardez*

Act I
The Story Begins

Scene One: Ring

Sophie enters and speaks directly to you.

I am 29 years old, washing dishes in a rented run-down three-bedroom row house in a small Canadian town. Ruth is at junior kindergarten; Dora is drooling beside me in an ExerSaucer. The phone rings. I dry my hands and answer the phone.

> Hello?
>
> > Is Joe there?

It's a woman, around my age.

> > He's away on business until next week.
> > Can I take a message?
>
> > > Who's this?

That's rude.

> > This is his wife. (*Pause.*) Can I help you?
>
> > > Are you serious? You can't be.

I put one hand on the counter.
I am using my best reasonable voice.

> > I have been for ten years. He lives here.
> > We have two children.
>
> > > Oh my God.

11

Can I help you?

Now I am irritated.

I'm his fiancée.

The room is very still. Even the baby is quiet.

I'm afraid you must be mistaken. Would you like to
leave a message?

Oh my God.

She hangs up. The winter sun is kissing the geraniums in
the kitchen window. I call my husband. I can't reach him. I can
never reach him when he goes away, no matter how many times
I ask him to make sure his cell phone works. I continue washing
the dishes.

Later, he calls. He sighs. He meant to tell me. There's a men-
tally unbalanced woman named Angel who works at one of the
companies he's been visiting. She's delusional, stalking him, and
he's going to have to speak to her boss about it. He's been putting
it off because he feels bad for her and doesn't want her to get the
sack. I believe him.

Three days later, she calls again. I am boiling pasta; the kids
are watching a *Maisy* movie.

Hello?

I am so sorry. *(She is in tears.)* I am sorry
to call, I won't do it again, I just wanted to
say I am so sorry, I had no idea.

Can I help you?

I am impervious, the matron of a psych ward.

You don't understand.

I understand perfectly. I'm sorry, you seem very
distressed.

Oh, my God, you don't believe me.

What I believe or don't believe is not your concern. I
understand you believe it.

> He bought me a ring, he sends
> me money. He said he was divorced.

> I'm so sorry.

I don't remember the rest of the conversation. I am cold,
barely polite. I treat her as if she is crazy. She *is* crazy, almost
hysterical. I eventually hang up. My hands are shaking. He
never bought *me* a ring. It's not true, I decide. So it isn't.

Scene Two: Tissues

I am in a group working on a community festival for International
Women's Day. I have written and directed a play based on the
group's priorities and experiences. It is a stupendously successful
show, offering a gritty, funny look at small-town married life. It
is particularly hilarious because I have cast my own husband as
the bad partner, the passive-aggressive, dishonest, philandering,
narcissistic bastard who dies on stage. He plays the role brilliantly.
I am so grateful for his support. We're such a great couple.

We strike the set and go home, but something is wrong. An
avalanche is coming from somewhere inside me. I can't sleep in
his bed. Then I can't sleep on the couch. Then I can't even *look*
at him. Please, he cries. Don't do this to the kids. Be careful, he
yells. I'll give you fifty bucks, keep the girls, and kick your ass to
the curb. I leave him.

I go to the shelter's outreach office, to ask if I've been abused.
A stout, friendly woman, the kind who drinks diet soda all day
and collects teddy bears, opens the bulletproof door. She gives
me a highlighter and a legal size piece of paper, thickly printed
on both sides with various abusive behaviors. It takes a long time
to send each question out like a sonar ping into the abyss. She
gives me her card, a handful of flyers, legal aid papers, housing
referral forms, and a hard candy. Call anytime, she says. It makes

no sense, even as I unfold the wads of memory, like nasty tissues left in coat pockets. The stories I cannot tell. I am afraid of making him angry, of not being believed, of my children reading awful things about their father.

I have written a play that has ruined or saved my life. When I have panic attacks, the man who will become my lover wraps me in a blanket, brings me clear sweet tea, and plays with the girls. I am a disgusting imposter. I don't understand. If only, I think, if only I could talk to that woman again. If only she could tell me what was really going on in my life. More than anything, I need to apologize for not believing her, for being so rude. I am so sorry.

But Angel doesn't call, and I cannot find her.

Scene Three: School

I have a Master's Degree in Canadian Studies, but have been a stay-at-home mom for eight years. In September the baby will start school. I have been earning a bit as a gardener and figure drawing model, but there is no work around here. I could probably get a job in the city, but the idea scares me and I don't want my freshly-traumatized kids to suddenly be in day-care full time. I need a better way to support my family. I visit a former professor, and she suggests I apply for the department's new PhD program. The deadline is four days away. Why not? What am I interested in? Recovery from spousal abuse. I am accepted, and the scholarships pay way better than welfare.

I am good at school; my brain knows all the tricks. I have run out of money for therapy. Surely here, in the books, I will find the decoder ring, the knowledge that makes sense of this mess called my life.

Sophie exits.

Act II
Asking Books

Scene One: Trauma

A hot pool roughly the size of two parking spots, at the local community center. Sophie is sitting on the edge in a black lap suit. The rest of the cast rolls and lolls in the chlorine froth like poached fish.

Sophie: Why didn't I DO anything about it sooner? Why didn't I LEAVE?

Kearney: You're committed. You want to save him, it's under control, it's not that bad, or it's at least partially your fault. Maybe it's tradition or religion. You can't see any options. You rationalize it.[1]

Metasophie: *(adjusting her bikini)* You're a dependent idiot.

Krystal: Surrender to what seems to be inevitable, inescapable, immediate danger, initiates an affective process of paralysis of initiative, followed by varying degrees of immobilization leading to automatic obedience.[2]

Metasophie: *(piling her curly brown hair in a loose bun on top of her head)* Isn't that convenient.

Swift: That's a prejudicial question, Sophie. Your choices are not the problem here.[3]

Sophie: But why am I still such a basket-case?

Metasophie sighs, slides down to rest her skull on the pool edge, closes her eyes and lets her body float.

Herman: Ordinary, healthy people can become entrapped in prolonged abusive situations, but after your escape you are no longer ordinary or healthy.[4]

Caruth: It's trauma, dear. A memory you cannot integrate into your experience, or a catastrophic knowledge you can't communicate to others.[5]

Metasophie: *(without opening her eyes)* We're a basket case because…because—

Ubersophie: *(standing by the pool edge, overheated and bare-foot, with her pants rolled up, speaking to Metasophie)* You don't know, so just shut up and let us think.

van der Kolk: You experience current stress as a return of the trauma.

van der Hart: Yes. Your 'alarm bell' is over-sensitive.[6]

Krystal: *(while examining an air bubble in his baggy trunks)* It causes cognitive constriction, episodic 'freezing,' inability to act assertively or aggressively, passivity or blundering, 'surrender' patterns when under stress, dread or avoidance of memories, numbing, hypervigilance, and the inability to feel joy or articulate emotions.[7] *(Smiles at Sophie and shrugs, spreading his hands.)* You're perfectly normal.

Ubersophie: Didn't I say?

Tutty: Also anxiety, nightmares, sleep and eating disorders.[8]

Herman: *(almost totally submerged, slowly bobbing in front of a jet)* Disconnection, alienation, shame, doubt, guilt, feelings of inferiority, oscillating intolerance to and outbursts of anger, self-isolation and clinging to others, suicidality, and depression.

Sophie: Great. *(to Ubersophie)* I can't feel it. Is it true?

Ubersophie: We're perfectly normal.

Metasophie: *(without opening her eyes)* Pathetic.

Herman: Protracted depression. Your identity is "contaminated with shame, self-loathing, and failure."[9]

Krystal: And despair, which, they've proven, can cause all sorts of physical ailments. Only a vestige of the self-observing ego is preserved.[10]

Sophie: That makes me sound so broken.

Erikson: You've lost the illusions of safety that make life seem manageable.

Ubersophie: Life *is* manageable. It has to be.

Erikson: The laws of the natural world and human decency have been revealed as false. You lose faith in the good will of others, in reason and logic, and often, in God. The real problem is that, over time, inhumanity starts to seem normal.[11]

Metasophie: Look around. Inhumanity *is* normal.

Kelly: Trauma also delays psychological maturation and memory integration.[12] So you're a little delayed.

Metasophie laughs.

Kelly: See, it produces a temporal paradox.

Sophie: This isn't Star Trek.

Kelly: No, listen. You've suffered a fundamental dislocation of time and space. It's fascinating.

Herman: Both the future and the past are eventually obliterated.[13]

Ubersophie: That excuses nothing. You still knew what you needed to do.

Metasophie: So what?

Ubersophie: *(to Metasophie)* You're not helping.

Metasophie: *(to Ubersophie)* Neither are you, standing there off-gassing shoulds as if that ever did us a damn bit of good.

Herman: *(sits up and shakes water out of her ears)* Honey. You've been entrapped by appeals to your most cherished values and your empathy for your abuser. Your history of affection for him. *(Sighs.)* It alters your personality. You get a kind of "atrophy in the psychological capacities that have been suppressed."[14]

Metasophie: *(to Ubersophie)* I like you better atrophied.

Ubersophie: *(to Metasophie)* Who're you calling atrophied? As if we listen to *you.*

Herman: Do you have many friends?

Sophie: Uh... no.

Metasophie: People are scary.

Ubersophie: We don't have time.

Herman: *(shaking her head)* Tsk. The over-development of a solitary inner life. It stinks, but there it is. All the signs of post-traumatic stress disorder.

Sophie: Really?

Metasophie: Again with the labels. Why does that make you so horny? Jesus.

Ubersophie: Cognitive frameworks can help.

Metasophie: Until you're hanging in them.

Sophie: I'm not comfortable with that...

Ristock: Rightly so. I'll grant that PTSD does name some of what women experience as symptoms, and that "can help lessen the self-blame. But it's a limited psychological framework that ignores women's subjective experiences of violence" and the complexity of its effects.[15] *(to Herman)* AND you're hogging the jet. Again.

Herman: *(to Ristock)* You'll get a turn when I'm done.

Ristock: *(pissy)* How feminist of you.

Young: Your response to oppression becomes a deficient personality trait—

Nadeau: Or a dysfunctional syndrome for the trauma industry to medicate and manage.[16]

Ubersophie: We could use the help.

Metasophie: In exchange for a label? No, thanks.

Ranck: You can't ignore the historical and political context. PTSD misses "an encounter with the moral and social imperatives that emerge from the wound. Traumatization becomes a pathological condition to be treated rather than an experiential knowledge demanding legitimation."[17] It's individualized and depoliticized.

Sophie: It does *feel* pretty personal.

Ristock: But that way of seeing it is disempowering. Your symptoms are framed as a betrayal of the body—external, outside of your control and involuntary.[18]

Herman: But they *are*. "The essential insult of trauma" is helplessness.[19]

(Ubersophie snorts. So does Ristock.)

Edkins: She's right. Powerlessness and betrayal of trust.

Ubersophie: No. We just didn't try hard enough.

Sophie: So how was I helpless?

Edkins: Someone you thought would protect you turned out to be dangerous.[20]

Ubersophie: *(to Metasophie)* If you weren't so bloody *emotional*—

Metasophie: Go ahead. Blame me. 'Cause *that's* rational.

Sophie: But I'm smart and strong and middle class, and he was just some poor wanna-be rock musician...

Ubersophie: What were you thinking?

Metasophie: Stupid.

Ubersophie: If we'd married up at least we'd have money.

Edkins: *(to Herman)* And you ARE hogging the jet.

Herman: *(sighs, moving over)* Through "disassociation, voluntary thought suppression, minimization, and sometimes outright denial," you learn to alter an unbearable reality.[21] It's Orwellian doublethink.

While Ristock and Edkins non-verbally sort out who will take the jet, Krystal, oblivious throughout, heaves himself in front of it and settles in with a contended sigh. Herman laughs.

Sophie: But—

Miller: The more hurt—

Stiver: —and violated—

Miller: —you're made to feel, the more you leap to the belief that *you*—

Stiver: —you're the bad one.[22]

Ubersophie: Short leap.

Landenburger: You internalize his view that you're useless without him and you blame yourself.[23]

Sophie: *(tucking her knees against her chest, looking at her toes)* I wanted him to like me.

Ubersophie: Idiot.

Sophie: Well I didn't do it on purpose.

Krystal: High self-expectations and low self-esteem. It's classic.

Metasophie: Low self-esteem, my ass.

Ubersophie: As if you aren't the most vain, self-absorbed, egotistical person I know.

Metasophie: Next to Joe.

Ubersophie: Not far off.

Sophie: *(to Meta and Uber)* Would you STOP.

Herman: *(patting Sophie's foot)* Honey, all traumatized people "search for faults in their own behavior in an effort to make sense of what has happened to them."[24]

Ubersophie: It has to make sense.

Metasophie: Good luck with that.

Sophie: But I really think—

Gillis: You were made to feel responsible for your own abuse—

Diamond: —and even to assist in covering up the abusive behavior.[25]

Ubersophie: Oh, for god's sake. What abuse?

Metasophie: It was my fault.

Miller: Women often come to believe deep down that they are unworthy—

Stiver: —because of the abuse they have suffered.[26]

Sophie: Maybe, but—

Kearney: You were just responding to "cultural and personal expectations for romance, service, and commitment."

Metasophie: Little Miss Frilly Apron.

Kearney: You experienced "changed perceptions of self and reality" in your violent relationship.[27]

Ubersophie: Violent how? Show me the evidence.

Sophie: But he never hit me.

Herman: Oh, so it's all right, then?

Sophie: No, but—

Gillis: He didn't *have* to hit you. Emotional stuff can be even worse.

Diamond: Any behavior or pattern of behavior used to coerce, dominate, or isolate your partner is abuse.[28]

Sophie: But how do I know if I dominated him?

Ubersophie: We did manage him. Constantly. Had to.

Metasophie: Of *course*. (*mocking*) That's what we *do*.

Ubersophie: If you weren't so pig-headed.

Metasophie: You're not stupid and weak enough to be a victim.

Ristock: I hear what you're saying. The "image of the victim as pure, innocent and helpless" looms so large in the dominant culture. There's no room for your agency, strength, resiliency, or even anger.[29]

Sophie: Yeah.

Ristock: At the same time, like anyone, you respond to the label "victim" with aversion.

Metasophie: They don't know what a nasty little thing we are, what an unloving, bossy piece of—

Ubersophie: Stop it.

Sophie: There's so much negative self-talk. How do you know if it's true?

Ristock: We blame victims because we don't want to believe it could happen to us.

Metasophie: We're not like other people. You know it.

Ubersophie: Of course not. We're—

Metasophie: What? *Special?*

Ristock: Most women sit somewhere in the middle. But victim and perpetrator get built as polar opposites: perps choose to act violently and are never understood in context; while victims are always already in a state of oppression and so can't be held accountable for their choices.[30]

Sophie: But I *know* I made choices.

Ubersophie: And his choices—

Metasophie: He—

Ubersophie: He's messed up, sure, but he's acting out learned patterns, just like us.

Sophie: Denying my agency just seems like a cheap way to absolve myself of all accountability. It's what he would do.

Swift: Of course you made choices, but they were determined by the sanctions and options you encountered—both internal and external.[31]

Ubersophie: How is he any different?

Sophie: *(a bit sullen)* I had power.

Metasophie: We'd rather be bad than weak.

Ristock: We assume that we'll find power and control as "the core features of an abusive relationship," and that women's thoughts and movements will be restricted by fear and intimidation. We over-simplify. The model isn't wrong, it just doesn't tell us much. Then women who don't fit get seen as being in denial or not real victims.[32]

Herman: But were you afraid?

Metasophie: Absolutely. Always.

Ubersophie: Never.

Sophie: I don't know. Sometimes.

Metasophie: How can you forget everything? It makes me look crazy for feeling anything.

Ubersophie: You are crazy. It was under control.

Metasophie: IT WAS SO NOT! I was terrified ALL THE TIME. When you pack it down where do you think it GOES?

Ubersophie: Pack what down?

Metasophie: Oh my GOD! *(to Sophie)* What about the time— what about when—um—that time in the car. That was messed up.

Sophie: *(sliding down into the pool, looking at nobody)* This one time we got home from somewhere. He parked and I wanted to go right in so the babysitter could go home. It was late, and it's five bucks an hour, you know?

Metasophie: So you're saying it was about the money?

Sophie: We were so broke. Five bucks was an hour of freedom. But he kept going on about how he loved me so much but I was so judgmental and incapable of love and it hurt him so bad and—you know.

Metasophie: Meanwhile he has a FUCKING SECRET PHONE LINE just for phone sex. You never say that part.

Ubersophie: It's embarrassing.

Metasophie: So you made me a liar. When the phone got cut off for three months 'cause he'd spent all the money talking smut. Calling his girlfriends.

Ubersophie: It's your own fault, for not putting out.

Sophie: *(quietly)* I actually believed his stupid explanations.

Ubersophie: I could have checked the bills. I should have known.

Metasophie: It wasn't the first time. It happened again and again. Like on that drive home from Toronto, all the way about how we never loved him like he loved us.

Ubersophie: Possibly true, but not in the way that he meant it.

Metasophie: I *did* love him. I *did*. And he *knew* it. I tried so *hard*.

Sophie: There was nothing I could say. It just got worse. So I'd just wait. That time it went on for, what? An hour?

Metasophie: More. I was shaking the whole time.

Ubersophie: It was cold. That's all.

Sophie: I could have said, look, this is crazy, and gone in.

Metasophie: No I couldn't!

Sophie: It was past eleven and I'd told the sitter we'd be home by ten. She had school the next day.

Ubersophie: He couldn't have stopped us. We chose to stay.

Metasophie: It would have got worse. Proof that we didn't care and weren't listening and he was right.

Ubersophie: We were okay.

Metasophie: Because you were *completely* disassociated. How is that okay?

Sophie: The door wasn't even locked. Was that fear? Stupidity? Was I just trying to be *nice*?

Metasophie: We were totally trapped. Cornered.

Ubersophie: We were listening. That's what partners do.

Ristock: Victims often express compassion for their abusers.[33]

Ubersophie: He was probably feeling some distress, too.

Metasophie: He used our compassion against us. He still does.

Sophie: I must have had a reason.

van der Kolk: Feelings of physical—

van der Hart: —or emotional paralysis—

van der Kolk: —are integral to traumatic experiences.[34]

Ubersophie: I could have walked away at any point.

Metasophie: As if it's that simple.

Ubersophie: Being a sex addict and jerk doesn't make him abusive.

Metasophie: Then WHY AM I SO SCARED? It was *so much more* than that.

Ubersophie: More what? Explain it, then.

Metasophie: I'm *trying.* I can't just—explain it all, as if it makes sense, like there's *evidence.* The little stories, like how he'd never sit facing me, they add up to nothing. And the big stories—

Ubersophie: You're pathetic.

Metasophie: What do you need me to say? What do I need to say? Do I have to tell you how, in bed—

Ubersophie: No.

Metasophie: I *can't go there.* This isn't Jerry Springer. These stories can *kill me.*

Ubersophie: You're getting hysterical.

Sophie: I just wanted it to stop. I think.

Metasophie: You needed him not to be angry and disappointed in you. So the babies were safe and everything was okay. And the only way to make that happen was to make yourself smaller and smaller until you disappeared. The only thing you could feel was sorry. Sorry I was too demanding and unforgiving and untrusting and big and smart and scary.

Ubersophie: Oh, you poor little thing.

Metasophie: He wanted to *own* me.

Ubersophie: You spent too much time in Women's Studies.

Metasophie: He even said that *he made me a writer.* That I'd be
    nothing without him. When I *knew* I was a writer since
    I was *four years old.* I am SO ANGRY—

Sophie: *(shrugs)* I don't remember.

*The theorists in the pool look at one another, trying to find
something to say. Sophie is still looking down into the water.
Edkins nudges van der Kolk, who mumbles briefly with van der
Hart, then clears his throat nervously.*

van der Kolk: "Severe or prolonged stress can suppress hip-
    pocampal functioning, creating context-free fearful
    associations—"

van der Hart: *(nodding)* "which are hard to locate in space and
    time."

van der Kolk: "This results in amnesia for the specifics of trau-
    matic experience but not the feelings associated with
    them."[35]

Sophie: So I forget things.

Brison: *(flushed and agitated)* You lose your memories and your
    ability to envision a future. Your basic cognitive and
    emotional capacities are gone, or radically altered. It's a
    total epistemological crisis.[36]

Ubersophie: I know what I know.

Metasophie: Oh, please.

Sophie: Like I forgot I went to court.

Ubersophie: That was a nuisance.

Metasophie: You wouldn't tell anyone.

Sophie: He hadn't paid the insurance or renewed the plates, but
    he lied and said he did.

Metasophie: Tell them what really happened.

Ubersophie: This is undignified.

Metasophie: Come on. You didn't know about the insurance. But you knew about the plates.

Ubersophie: It just makes us look bitter and petty.

Metasophie: You'd been asking for weeks. Did he get the new sticker. You're standing in the doorway. You say.

Sophie: Did you renew the plates?

Metasophie: You know you're nagging and he's going to be mad. And he says.

Sophie: I already told you I did. If you don't trust me then go and check.

Metasophie: *If you don't trust me.*

Sophie: Checkmate.

Metasophie: You would not look. You deliberately walked around the front of the car and *did not look*. Because then you'd have to deal with it.

Ubersophie: If you hadn't been so weak, it wouldn't have happened.

Sophie: Then, of course, I got pulled over.

Metasophie: I was so scared. Crying in the cruiser with no answers for the cop. I told him how I was stuck and asked him what I should do. He said nothing. I've never seen a person with such flat affect. *(to Ubersophie)* You'd have loved him.

Sophie: I'd never been to court. I went and got an outfit from the second hand store—a moss green knit suit.

Ubersophie: Practical.

Metasophie: Ugly.

Sophie: Afterwards I threw it out and literally, totally forgot about it for three years. Even once I remembered, I forgot again.

Metasophie: See? We're NOT OKAY.

Sophie: If a friend told me her memory did that, I'd say, whoa. Red flag. So maybe... But I could just be forgetful, you know?

Laub: That's what happens. There was no unencumbered, unviolated, sane point of reference for insider witnesses. You could not bear witness to yourself.

Sophie: I guess.

Ubersophie: What are the kids up to? We really should be out there playing with the girls. You never make any time for them.

Metasophie: Fuck it.

Ubersophie: That's nice. Very nice. They're going to remember how selfish you are.

Metasophie: I have nothing left inside.

Ubersophie: They're running by the pool. D'you know how dangerous that is? We should be watching them. They could drown. It happens all the time. You think you have guilt *now.*

Laub: This loss of the capacity to witness from the inside is "per- haps the true meaning of annihilation, because when your history is abolished, identity ceases to exist as well."[37]

Metasophie: *(to Sophie)* Could you PLEASE STOP THINKING? Who are these freaks? They don't even TALK like human beings. Can we not have a MOMENT of peace alone in the hot pool without you inviting all these freaking morons into our head?

Sophie: Great. I don't even exist. *(blows out air to lie on the bottom of the pool)*

Metasophie: That's better.

A long silence. Sophie is feeling the jets of water, bubbles and turbulence, lifting and pushing on her limbs, her pulse in her ears. A great crushing fatigue, heavier than the water, presses down on her chest. She feels small and calm.

Metasophie: *(whispers)* We could just stay here. Please.

Ubersophie: Don't be ridiculous.

Metasophie: *(to Ubersophie)* Shhh.

O'Neill: Don't blame yourself. Memories of trauma both beg to be forgotten and cry out to be remembered.[38]

Metasophie: *(to Ubersophie)* Ah, you bitch, you got her thinking again.

Caruth: You're carrying an impossible history.[39]

Sophie: *(surfacing, getting her goggles off the edge)* But where do memories *go*?

Levy: Your trust of memory and language has been so impaired by trauma that the very act you are trying to bring to justice renders you unable to do so.[40] It's a different empirical world.

Ubersophie: No it isn't.

van der Kolk: Trauma memories are generally unconscious—

van der Hart: —precise and somatic.

Metasophie: THANK you.

van der Kolk: They appear as behavioral reenactments—

van der Hart: —nightmares and flashbacks—

van der Kolk: —and are not easily expressed in language.[41]

Ubersophie: You're just acting out.

Sophie: So, I'm what—repressed? Crazy? Stupid? *(fiddling with goggles)*

Naples: That's exactly what Mary Gilfus was worrying about. These guys treating trauma like an individual psychological response that is ultimately constructed and diagnosed as psychopathology.[42] You're not crazy, Sophie. You're hurt.

Ubersophie: Oh, for GOD's sake.

Sophie: But couldn't you say the same thing about him? I'm sure he'd come up with some sob story to justify every shitty thing he ever did, or 'forgot'...

Ubersophie: Nice feminist ethic of care.

Mann: Bear in mind that "virtually all who provided testimony to the lived reality of abuse described an all-encompassing emotional sickness that threatens to entrap, to engulf, all participants."[43]

Sophie: You said ALL participants?

Mann: Er... right.

Sophie: So then, what? We're both sick?

Mann: But *he* has the control drive.

Sophie: He'd beg to differ.

Molly, a petite woman in her fifties with short grey hair and a flamingo-print swimming dress, enters the pool.

Molly: But, Sophie, lying is an act of violence. Did you lie?

Metasophie: Yes.

Ubersophie: No.

Sophie: *(shrugs)* I don't know. Sometimes.

Krystal smiles at Molly and moves over, giving her the best jet. She smiles back and sits, with great composure.

Molly: On purpose to hurt or control?

Sophie: I don't think so, but—

Ubersophie: How can you not know?

Metasophie: I don't know, I don't know, it's all a big blur, all I know is that I feel bad.

Molly: And did he?

Sophie: I don't know.

Metasophie: YES.

Ubersophie: YES.

Sophie: Maybe. But why would he?

Molly: That depends on how you look at it.

Mann: In the family violence model, the problem is damaged selves, male and female, trapped in mutual, often inter-generationally patterned cycles of abuse and dependency, based on risky situations, histories, attitudes, and behaviors. In the violence against women model, it's about using violence, coercion and intimidation to maintain male dominance.[44]

Metasophie: Oh, for chrissakes, who cares?

Mann: They're competing myths.

Molly: They both go back to fear of powerlessness.

Gillis: The abuse is tailor-made.

Diamond: Fitted to your specific vulnerabilities.[45]

Ubersophie: I am so disappointed in you.

Martz: You don't need to be embarrassed, Sophie.

Saraurer: Trying to please your partner is a common coping strategy.[46]

Sophie: You end up doing…

Molly: It's okay. We know.

The girls appear at the pool side, dripping. Ruth, at 10, is tall, lean and mischievous. Dora is a stocky, curly-topped, irrepressible 8 year old.

Ubersophie: Incoming!

Dora: Mom! MOM! You've GOT to go down the slide! It's AWESOME!

They splash into the hot pool.

Sophie: Hey, girls.

Dora: *(bouncing)* Come ON!

Sophie: *(snippy)* I HEARD you.

Metasophie: *(tenderly)* These are my babies.

Dora is a little crestfallen. Ruth slips into Sophie's lap and pats her face.

Ruth: Whatcha doing?

Sophie: Just thinking. Okay. *(takes a breath)* Okay. *(dumps Ruth off her lap)* Let's go.

Dora: YEAH!

Metasophie: *(to Ubersophie)* You're gonna get wet. *(smiles)*

Scene Two: Haunting

An unfinished, long narrow space. At one end, a desk; at the other, an enormous heap of laundry. Sophie is sitting at the desk, writing. She stands, pauses to write on a post-it: Is spousal abuse colonial? and crosses to the laundry. She turns on the radio and starts folding and sorting. A cream-colored curly-coated puppy sleeping nearby lifts her head to listen.

Radio Host:

Good evening. Tonight on Ideas: This Haunted Land. Sophie Tamas on memory, trauma, and the Canadian identity. Many Canadian cultural producers seem almost obsessed with trauma, as revealed through the trope of haunting.[47] This trope offers empowering stories of "loss, rupture, recovery, healing and wisdom" and is "at its core, political. It provokes (and insists upon) questions about ownership, entitlement, dispossession, and voice" while challenging false dualities of self and other, inside versus outside.[48] Haunting confronts us with our "buried or forgotten history and the necessity of being led somewhere, elsewhere."[49]

The foundational trauma of our settler-invader society has produced a rich body of haunted Canadian literature. Tonight, Carleton University's Sophie Tamas takes us through Canadian gothic and magic realist work, which represents the unspeakable by accessing the spiritual, mystical, or supernatural.[50] This work reckons with ghosts as everyday figures of memory,[51] calling us to "change our way of seeing or apprehending experience."[52] In many Canadian stories, haunting and magic allow us to read tragedy under the comic sign of the Trickster.[53] But Tamas warns, such stories can also exploit and romanticize trauma, as an envied source of cultural depth, while containing past horrors and positioning the present as a happy ending.[54] Our ghost stories may be a melancholy, narcissistic attempt to forget the impossible.[55]

Sophie: *(on the radio)*

We begin with Derrida. "There has never been," he says, "a scholar who really, and as a scholar, deals with ghosts. A traditional scholar does not believe in ghosts—nor in all that could be called the virtual space of spectrality. There has never been a scholar who, as such, does not believe in the sharp distinction between the real and the unreal, the actual and the inactual, the living and the non-living, being and non-being…in the opposition between what is present and what is not, for example, in the form of objectivity. Beyond this opposition, there is, for the scholar, only the hypothesis of a school of thought, theatrical fiction, literature, and speculation."[56]

Sophie turns off the radio.

Sophie: *(to the puppy)* What a load of crap.

The puppy smiles and nods, then settles her chin on her paws. Sophie crosses back to the desk. A moth flies over her shoulder and lands. She picks up an empty glass and lowers it, upside down, over the moth. Sits, watching. Adds to the post-it note: Am I haunted? Carefully slides the glass onto a piece of paper, and exits, carrying the moth. The puppy follows, her tags softly jingling.

Scene Three: Recovery

Molly's office. Sophie sits cross-legged on a blue couch, hands in her lap, absently kneading a tissue. Molly sits opposite, in an office chair, with a large glass of water on a small stool beside her. The carpet is pale pink; the artwork is local; there is an enameled faux wood stove in the corner.

Molly: How are you doing?

Sophie: Oh, I don't know. Not too bad, but between school, kids, and working on the house. You know. We discovered all the studs have rotted out against the stone foundation so I've pulled up all the floors around the exterior walls and spent all week breaking up the foundation and hauling out rocks so we can lay new pressure-treated footings and beams and sister the floor joists and reframe the house so it's properly supported. Which, of course, means stripping everything down. Tearing out the plaster and lathe and taking off the sheathing—which is all horizontal pine planks, up to two feet wide. And the walls are full of sawdust—which has to be hauled out in wheelbarrows. And Shawn's freaking out about his job, which is, of course, stressing me out, too. So. Same old, same old. *(smiles weakly)*

Molly: That's a lot to manage.

Sophie: It's still not heated, and Shawn's pulled all the plumbing, so thank god we've still got the old place. But it's tough with the kids. They help, but—

Molly: How're they doing?

Sophie: Alright. They've adjusted really well to being a blended family, and Tahirh is actually starting to trust me—

Molly: She's fourteen?

Sophie: Yeah.

Molly: Tough age. She gets on well with Ruth and Dora?

Sophie: Amazingly. We've had her full time for a couple years now, but her mom issues are still huge.

Molly: Lots of transition going on.

Sophie: They're all super high-need. Ruth and Dora come home from weekends at their dad's completely messed up. Neither ex really pays child support, so we're crazy broke. And then there's school, of course. Teaching and reading and writing and blah blah blah.

Molly: And how are you?

Sophie: I'm okay. There just isn't enough of me to go around. But I'm liking the dog.

Molly laughs.

Sophie: I never had a dog before. Cricket is great.

Molly: Yeah.

Sophie: It depends which part of me you're talking about. Parts of me function really well. It's just not integrated.

Molly: Kind of like a split, inside?

Sophie: Sure. You have to, to get things done. *(sighs)* Do you think that I'm haunted?

Molly: *(smiling)* That's a great question. What do you think?

Sophie: I don't know. I've been thinking about Angel. *(changes direction)* I was reading this thing in Anne Michaels's *Fugitive Pieces.* She said the ghosts which haunt the traumatized whisper, not for us to join them, but so that we get close enough for them to push us back out into the world.[57] *(Molly waits.)* Do you think I'm recovering?

Molly laughs.

Molly: I don't know. It can feel like "you've landed beyond the moral universe, beyond the realm of predictable events and comprehensible actions, and you don't know how to get back."[58]

Sophie: Exactly.

Molly: Trauma can be like a nonsensical entry in the sequence of your life. Whatever trajectory your life is on, after that, might not seem to be one of recovery. There might be no discernable pattern. I remember one therapist telling me it's precisely because you're doing so well that you're feeling so much worse.[59]

Sophie: That helps.

Molly: *(laughs)* Yeah. I was like, are you *kidding* me? *Man.*

Sophie: But if you can't feel yourself getting better, how do you keep going? How do you even know if you're going in the right direction?

Molly: I don't know. I think you've got to wager or will yourself to believe that the future might hold pleasure as well as agony, right? There never was a coherent self, things never did make sense. You've got to "reestablish the illusory sense of the permanence of hope."[60]

Sophie: So, be delusional.

Molly: I don't think you can will yourself to believe something you know to be false. But you can, to some extent, piece your shattered assumptions of safety back together.

Sophie: Do you think we get better?

Molly: It depends what you mean by better. I do see people change. Sometimes things happen that seemed impossible.

Sophie: I was reading this Holocaust survivor, Jean Amery. He said, "Whoever was tortured, stays tortured."[61]

Molly: I don't know. Have you read Joan Didion?

Sophie: No.

Molly: She's written a book about the death of her partner, where she talks about how she could not imagine or prepare for the unending void. It felt like the opposite of meaning. The relentless succession of moments in

which she confronted the experience of meaningless-
ness itself.[62] Which made it really difficult to present a
coherent face to the world.[63] But at the same time, she's
written a book about it. So she *has* made sense of it, in
some way.

Sophie: It just feels like, what, *still?* Like I should be over it. Like
nothing is wrong.

Molly: Recovery can be a lifelong process with unclear chanc-
es of success.[64]

Sophie: I've been reading all these recovery do-lists. It's totally
demoralizing. Take someone like Karen Landenburger,
right? She says you've got to grieve the loss of the
relationship, and your dreams for it. But if you grieve
openly, people assume you miss the abuse.

Molly: You might not miss the abuse, but you could easily miss
the abuser. Or at least parts of him. Your hopes.

Sophie: But my life is so much better now. I bought a house, for
god's sake. On scholarships. I always wanted to have a
house, but I never even imagined I could buy one for
myself. How feminist is that?

Molly: It's a big accomplishment.

Sophie: I've got so many reasons to be happy.

Molly: You do. But the past is always there, hey? Affecting
your reactions to life and other people.[65]

Sophie: I know you've got to put it in the past. But you can't
very well do that when he's in your face almost every
day with emails or picking up the kids or whatever.

Molly: It's hard to make that separation.

Sophie: It never bloody ends. Telling me I need to recognize
and accept what happened and give up on self blame
and believe in myself just seems like a bunch of pious
crap.[66] It may be completely right. But if it was that
easy I wouldn't be here, would I?

Molly: And where is here?

Sophie: Totally stuck, right?

Molly: Hmmm.

Sophie: And maybe the problem *is* me. It's been four years. Maybe there *is* no massive unending head game power trip.

Molly: But you still don't feel safe.

Sophie: I know he can't actually hurt me. But he can *always* get to me, because of the kids. And it's not even that. It just doesn't make sense. *I* don't make sense. And that's what all the theorists pin their hopes on. Like Hannah Arendt says, "The outrageous requires not only lamentation and denunciation, but also comprehension."[67]

Molly: And it can be different things, hey, making sense with your head versus how it feels in your body.

Sophie: Completely. It's like I have three different people inside me.

Molly: You know, the way I understand it, that's really normal. The main difference between so-called healthy people and people we might diagnose with multiple personality disorder is how much conscious control we have over who's in charge, inside. How split off those voices are from each other.

Sophie: But if I *can* make sense then I *should* make sense, and if I can't then it has to be my fault.

Molly: That self-blame piece, hey? That can be a really powerful voice. Making sense takes a lot of courage. A determined willingness to bear the burden of events and face the facts unflinchingly.

Sophie: *(incredulous)* So it's about courage and will? My lack of courage and will?

Molly: Do you feel like that's the problem?

Sophie: No. I think I tried really hard.

Molly: Yeah. You sure did.

Sophie is on the edge of tears.

Sophie: I think I was really brave. Sometimes, anyhow. I tried to be.

Molly lets Sophie sit with her feelings, quietly, for a moment.

Molly: Do you think there could be a way to make sense of it where you don't deny or explain it away, but you just face it? An "unpremeditated, attentive facing up to, and resisting of, reality"?[68]

Sophie: But that assumes there *is* one knowable reality. And so often it seems like the real project is about making excuses. As if everything happened for a reason and nothing could have happened any other way.

Molly: I have seen a kind of understanding come. It seems both possible and necessary.[69]

Sophie: I know we're supposed to go through tough things and come out the other end strong and knowledgeable and whole.[70] But I don't *see* it. I want it to be true. But I can't map this mess to that grid.

Molly: Yeah.

Sophie: And it leaves so much out. Like, where do women abusers fit in that system? They don't.

Molly: Maybe you can't make sense of it or change the past, but you can change its meaning for you.

Sophie: How?

Molly: Well, not by simply desiring or deciding not to be burdened by it. That sure doesn't work.

Sophie: I wish.

Molly: If it was that easy I'd be out of work. Not by abstracting our interests in past actions, or forgetting.[71] But maybe sometimes there's a way to act unpredictably, to "upset expectations based on what you appear to be in order to reveal who you are becoming."[72]

Sophie: But is that really going to help?

Molly: I don't know.

Sophie: *Nobody* seems to know what helps.[73] Sure, they make lists. Release your anger and guilt, grow your independence and forgiveness, rediscover yourself, find purpose in life, feel self compassion, stand on your head and spit nickels.[74]

Molly: There hasn't actually been much focus on "the needs of women after they have left an abusive relationship and how they recover."[75]

Sophie: It's all about fixing *me*.

Molly: The question of how to recover gets "hopelessly muddled and ridden with moral judgment."[76] There are stages, but they're not tidy and sequential. You need safety, you need to remember and mourn, and you need to reconnect with ordinary life. But "recovery is never complete."[77]

Sophie: Do you know how much I have spent on therapy? I have gone to the freaking food bank so I could pay for this. Do you know how *humiliating* that is?

Molly: That's a hard place.

Sophie: Hard? *(laughs)* I think what I'd just like to know is, why. Why me? And I'll never know. I'll never know if he actually loved me, at any point, or if everything, every minute of it, was all a lie. I don't know which is worse. And the most awful part, the thing I can't get over, is the times when he was kind. The silly games or songs he used to sing. His being *nice* to me is the most dangerous thing of all. Even now. And I understand why, like Judith Herman says, you've got to reconstruct a system of belief that makes sense of your undeserved suffering.[78] But I have no place in my world for this kind of thing. What he did could not happen on my planet. I can't even *see* it. So I *have* no system of belief

40

anymore. It's *failed*. And you can't just go pick up a new one at the mall.

Molly: Sometimes you find meaning by looking beyond yourself.[79]

Sophie: Being less self centered. *(flops back on couch)* Perfect.

Molly: Sometimes, activism can be part of the healing. Like the work you're doing with your dissertation.

Sophie: But this so-called survivor mission can also be a really neat avoidance strategy. A way to intellectualize and externalize and stay obsessed with your losses without actually ever doing anything to let that shit go.

Molly: But you're here. It's not all or nothing.

Sophie: I *get* the need for a social reading. That survivors get turned into agents of patriarchal oppression, telling powerful stories of our own badness and failure instead of framing the problem as evidence of what's wrong out there in the world. Sure. I can see how that's true for other women. But it doesn't *feel* true to me. It doesn't *feel* like false consciousness to say if only I tried harder I could have this under control.[80] I've got way too much privilege to be a victim.

Molly: Back to that imposter thing, hey?

Sophie: And you know what really makes me nuts? They all say the cure is *connection*. You've got to connect with other women to see you're not uniquely flawed.[81] As if connection is inherently benign and all we really need is a good group.

Molly: Groups can really help counter the notion that you deserved your abuse, or are alone in it, and they do offer a forum for problem-solving.[82]

Sophie: Sure.

Molly: They make a space for untangling the complex web of everyday life and rehearsing performances of alternative realities.[83] Lots of studies show that they help with self-esteem, anger, and depression.[84] And you get to try on new interpretations of your identity and needs.[85] But how do you feel about them?

Sophie: I HATE groups.

Molly laughs.

Sophie: That probably makes me a bad feminist. But I have tried. I did the coloring; I did the affirmations and the worksheets. I ate the snacks. I've sat through groups where one of them was currently shacked up with another one's abuser. I have listened. I have *shared.* But I can't just say what I think, oh no, because then they look at me like I have three heads, because they don't understand the words I am using, or I am dumping my cynicism all over the nicey-nicey bullshit that gives them hope. I have no idea what it's like to be 20 years old with four kids by four different men, all of whom are wards of the state, and be sitting in a survivor's group pregnant with number five. Or to hear the voices of your dead parents, or let your cop husband beat the shit out of you, even though you're a black belt and could kick his ass, because you'll lose your job if you're charged with assault. I don't know how these people get through the day. And I am happy to listen to them. But if I open my mouth, if I don't be small and quiet, they all shut down. The whole tragically futile, pathetically hopeless charade of getting better together fails. Somehow, that's got to be my problem. Clearly, I am doing something wrong. Maybe I'm projecting, maybe I'm afraid, I don't know. It's supposed to help. Maybe it's helping. Maybe it's all in my head. Honestly, the most useful thing I ever got from a women's group, or therapy group, or mindfulness group, or whatever, was a pair of slippers.

Molly: There's a lot of feelings there.

Sophie: It probably just shows what a narcissistic, shitty human being I am. My bad.

Molly: Well— *(smiling, neatly folding her small hands)* We'll pick up here next week. Okay?

Scene Four: Sex

A king size mattress on a low platform. Sophie sits down on the bed, naked. Shawn rolls toward her. He is blonde and so burly that she looks small beside him.

Shawn: How was Molly?

Sophie: *(pulls a nightshirt from under her pillow, turns it right side out)* Eh. You know.

Shawn: *(lifts the covers, pulls her down to spoon)* That good?

Sophie: I'm reading this book on writing by Bud Goodall.[86]

Shawn: *(stroking her belly)* Mmm?

Sophie: Somehow I'm supposed to give the reader chills AND goosebumps AND make them cry AND laugh AND make the world a better place AND not be self indulgent.

Shawn: *(stroking her hip)* Mmmm.

Sophie: So far I'm forty pages in, and it's all depressing. Me-me-me. *(sighs)* I'm going to lose the reader.

Shawn: Throw in a sex scene.

Sophie: *(laughs)* I can't do that.

Shawn: Always gets *my* attention.

Sophie: You're not on my committee.

Shawn: Just shake your bon bons *(gently bouncing her breast in his hand)*.

Sophie: *(laughs)* Yeah. Like that'll work.

Shawn: *(stroking her head)* You'll be fine. Who's my lion?

Sophie: *(meekly, playing)* Meow?

Shawn: *(kissy noises, tickling her thighs)* Here, puss puss puss....

Sophie: ROAR!

Shawn: There it is.

Sophie: Goofy. It's like David Mamet said. In the second act it all comes undone and you lose your way and fall into despair and then somehow the real goal of the quest is revealed.[87]

Shawn: *(massaging her back)* Hmm. And do I come galloping to the rescue?

Sophie: *(snorts)* This isn't really a play. It's probably everything Mamet hates. It should be in the first act you set out with some high-minded goal. In the second act you realize you were arrogant and wrong but you somehow create the will to continue. Strength and will. To face your own character, turn despair into some higher resolve, whatever. D'you know Tolstoy said if you don't undergo this revision sometime in your thirties, the rest of your life will be intellectually sterile?[88]

Shawn: Despair. You should nail that.

Sophie: *(smacks him)* Bugger. *(sighs)* It's too manipulative and rational.

Shawn: Remember what Sarah said. Aim for defendable.

Sophie: I know, I know. *(pause)* So what have you been thinking about? Sir Thomas Moore? Gilgamesh?

Shawn: No.

Sophie: The big bang?

Shawn: Warmer.

Sophie: *(nuzzling in)* Lemon meringue.

Shawn: Go hang.

Sophie: Wu-tang. *(turns to kiss him)* Good night.

Sophie sits up to pull on her nightshirt.

Shawn: That's it? *(snorts)* You will *definitely* lose your reader.

Sophie lies down. A sudden vacuum opens in her belly; her skin has not moved, but there is nobody left inside it.

Shawn: *(putting a hand on her belly)* Baby.

Sophie: *(in a small voice)* I'm okay.

Shawn: *(rolling her into a blanket cocoon)* What happened?

Sophie says nothing, does not move.

Shawn: I didn't even ASK. If I can't even WANT—

Sophie: I'm sorry. It's okay.

Shawn: We have to be able to—

Sophie: I know. We can.

Shawn: I love the way we are together, you KNOW that. But if I even HINT—you disappear. And then I can't—

Sophie: I know.

Shawn: It chases you away.

Sophie starts to tremble.

Shawn: Baby. Don't go down the rabbit hole. You're safe.

Sophie: Sorry.

Shawn: What am I supposed to do?

Sophie: You're not doing anything wrong.

Shawn: If it's not YOUR idea, I never know—

Sophie: *(starting to panic)* I just didn't—'cause we just had—and I wasn't—

Shawn: *(on his back, hands on his stomach, eyes closed, interrupting gently)* Alright. It's okay. Goodnight.

Long pause. Sophie rolls toward Shawn and puts a hand tentatively on his shoulder.

Shawn: I know you love me. Put your earplugs in and go to sleep. *(kisses her hand and tucks it back under her covers)*

Long pause. Shawn listens. Once Sophie is fully asleep, he quietly gets out of bed. Metasophie lifts her head and watches him go.

Scene Five: Play

Dora is sitting at Sophie's desk, reading the beginning of the previous scene, on her laptop. She has bed-head and is wearing a rumpled night shirt. Sophie enters from the bathroom, hands full of dirty laundry, naked.

Sophie: *(startled)* Whatcha doing?

Dora: This is funny.

Sophie: You like it? *(puts laundry in the hamper)*

Dora: Yeah. I didn't realize you were writing a play. I thought you were just writing. Am I in it?

Sophie: Yeah.

Dora: It's funny. *(smiling; she follows Sophie into the bathroom)* What am I doing?

Sophie: Drooling. And splashing. It's not a big part.

Dora laughs.

Dora: Drooling?

Sophie: You're a baby.

Dora: Oh. Can I be in it?

Sophie: *(turning on the shower)* It's not going to be performed.

Dora: Oh.

Sophie: But someday I'll write a play you can be in.

Dora: Okay. *(smiles, starts loading her toothbrush)* What's it for?

Sophie: My dissertation.

Dora: *That's* your dissertation?

Sophie: Yeah.

Dora: A *play?*

Sophie: Well, sort of. *(getting into the shower)* It's not supposed to be.

Dora: What's it supposed to be?

Sophie: About how or if women recover from spousal abuse.

Dora: Oh. *(starts brushing teeth, pauses, considering)* I think they'll like it.

Scene Six: Testimony

A small lecture hall on campus.

Ubersophie: Today we will be talking about testimony, the act of representing your experience.

According to Eli Wiesel, testimony is the characteristic genre of our era.[89] Felman explains that testimony "seems to be composed of bits and pieces of a memory that has been overwhelmed by occurrences that have not settled into understanding or remembrance, acts that cannot be construed as knowledge nor assimilated into full cognition, events in excess of our frames of reference."[90] It is implicated in almost every form of writing and "has become a crucial mode of our relation to the events of our times."[91] Testimony appears in a range of discourses, but today we'll look at three of its uses: as recovery, as social activism, and as remembrance.

Many therapists and some researchers see testimony as integral to personal healing from trauma. Traumatic experiences that you are unable or unwilling to narrate become distorted, pervasively invade and contaminate your daily life and may even be "incorporatively passed down to subsequent generations."[92] As Sophie Levy argues, "The release of the voice ensures survival...

escape is only possible... by repetition of events in language."[93] Not telling a story perpetuates its tyranny,[94] while telling in vivid emotional and bodily detail heals survivors, releases creative energy, converts traumatic memory into narrative memory, and reconnects us to others and to time.[95]

Some argue that testimony heals by enabling us to establish relational connections. Our losses are irredeemable, but we need not carry them in isolation.[96] Others suggest that testimony works by reconstituting an inner witness. This enables us to reintegrate and accept the othered aspects of ourselves, and, by extension, the otherness of others in the world.[97]

In theory, we can do this work on the page as well as face to face. Testimonial or autoethnographic writing can get us to places where we can feel hope, stimulate recovery, lead us into tales we can't quite remember, or help us deal with what has happened.[98] The past becomes a scrapbook that can safely be opened.[99] Healing is sometimes even attributed to testimonial writing about other people.[100] My own doctoral work is a sort of test of these claims.

Many feminist researchers, therapists and activists agree with most of the preceding, but argue that the point is social change as well as personal healing. Trauma narratives enable us to empathize with the life stories of others, which can lead us to examine and act on social problems.[101] They reveal "the contingency of the social order and in some cases how it conceals its own impossibility. They question our settled assumptions about who we might be as humans and what we might be capable of."[102] They offer what Jan Patocka calls "the solidarity of the shaken."[103] If "my pain or my silence or my anger or my perception is finally not mine alone... it delimits me in a shared cultural situation which in turn enables and empowers me in certain unanticipated ways."[104] This opens up trauma as an opportunity for structural analysis and collective activism. As bell hooks describes,

> Moving from silence to speech is for the oppressed, the colonized, the exploited, and those who stand and struggle side by side a gesture of defiance that heals, that makes new life

and new growth possible. It is the act of speech, of 'talking back,' that is no mere gesture of empty words, that is the expression of our movement from object to subject—the liberated voice.[105]

The third use of testimony is to support public remembrance. In this mode, testimony is entirely about its collective impact. It appears in two common forms. As a strategic, memorial pedagogy, it is used as a moral lesson, in the consolatory (if futile) hope of preventing future injustices. As a difficult return, it confronts us with the necessity and difficulty of living with irredeemable loss.[106] These public testimonies offer a counter-memory which confronts current norms and recognizes the oppressed and marginalized.[107] Their purpose is not to assist individual survivors of trauma, but rather to prevent the erasure of their experience in the dominant social narrative.

This form of testimony commonly underwrites the construction of monuments to commemorate sites of loss and suffering, from cenotaphs to impromptu roadside shrines, as well as memorial rituals and cultural productions. As Canadian playwright Judith Thompson explains, we write about trauma because "ultimately, as a culture, we can stop these things if we experience them, if we go through what other people have to go through."[108]

So those are three ways that we use trauma testimony. There are a number of questions or problems about testimony that I'd like to explore. The first is, how do we testify?

Language is part of the social order, so when the social order falls, so does language. "What we *can* say no longer makes sense; what we *want* to say, we can't. There are no words for it."[109] Susan Brison attributes this to "emotional illiteracy that prevents most people from conveying any feeling that can't be expressed in a Hallmark card."[110] We find trauma unspeakable; according to Homi Bhabha, this is because it is located outside of memory and text in an enunciatory void.[111] Brison contends that we have the words; we just find them unpleasant. Nonetheless, there is "an imperative to speak, and a determination to find ways of speaking that remain true to the trauma."[112]

This problem often leads away from the tidy specificity of positivist science and into the messier terrain of literary and artistic forms. Both the arts and social sciences seek shared cultural understanding through representation and interpretation.[113] But the arts may be much better suited to representing the emotional, embodied incoherence of catastrophe and pain.[114] Theodor Adorno argues that "it is now virtually in art alone that suffering can still find its own voice, consolation, without immediately being betrayed by it.... It is to works of art that has fallen the burden of wordlessly asserting what is barred to politics."[115] So we see scholarship about trauma written as poetic, generative, or performative texts.[116]

Any questions so far?

Metasophie: Is it all going to be okay? Will he finish the plumbing in time for me to install vapor barrier before the inspection so we can drywall before we have to move in? Can we live without walls? If testimony lets us accept othered parts of ourselves, why am I here? Is this healing or are you a meatpacker, selling off trimmed bits of us in Styrofoam and cellophane? Am I lost in the enunciatory void?

Ubersophie: No questions? Okay.

The second problem with testimony has to do with the issue of making sense. We tend to believe there is an anterior, definitive, singular, constant, passive reality 'out there,' which is independent of our actions and perceptions, and that things have causes.[117] We assume our life stories are linear, directional, cumulative and coherent; that the past explains the present (not vice versa), that contradictions are resolvable, and that there is a knowable, persistent self, a unified agent, sitting at the center of our stories.[118] Faced with inexplicable loss, we look for causes and reasons, justifications and explanations. Making trauma make sense is seen as a sign of recovery.[119]

The problem is that this modernist, teleological drive is tied to the "way of seeing, the way of being, the way of organizing human society" which is in large part responsible for the brutal situations many survivors must heal from.[120] As Melissa Orlie argues, the irrationality of the rational is one of the twentieth century's "gravest and most unnerving practical lessons."[121] Making sense takes a lot of editing and ignoring. We try to erase the experiences that don't fit.[122] Out there, it's oppression, colonialism, or objectification. Inside us, it's repression. Personally and socially, we are haunted by the return of the unassimilable otherness we repress in order to "make sense."[123]

We may read morals into our stories, simplifying the characters into evil villains and innocent victims, and re-casting ourselves as survivors in a culturally familiar tale of ennobling suffering which rewards us with grit and wisdom. The promise of post-traumatic growth offers us "something for which to be grateful, something to redeem the unmitigated awfulness."[124] Trauma is reframed as a sort of hard lesson, the romantic spice of a dull society. This makes it easier for us to live with the idea of suffering, our own and others', and easier to do nothing to prevent or minimize it.

If we presume that healing and recovery are possible and that post-traumatic growth balances the losses sustained, we can see those who remain traumatized as somehow wallowing, refusing to feel better, stubbornly and perversely clinging to their maladaptive coping mechanisms. We become irritated by their failure to recover because it threatens our need to believe in justice and the possibility of healing. The victims become the bearers of pathology— post-traumatic stress disorder, mental illnesses, eating disorders, sleep disorders, phobias, and addictions—and thus the focus of social intervention. This enables us to see suffering as an exceptional and perhaps deviant condition that we should and can get over within a "reasonable" amount of time. The world remains sensible. Our trauma stories are reframed as morbidly fascinating confessions subject to expert interpretation, and stripped of diversity, complexity, and subversive potential.[125]

Some scholars argue that postmodern and poststructural approaches open up a space in between the necessity and impossibility of ethically making sense. As Amy Novak explains, "Justice requires not the act of rationalizing, of constructing a smooth and logical account of this moment, but of remembering and maintaining contradictions."[126] They thus try to retain ambiguity and uncertainty in their work, without being completely incomprehensible.[127] They call into question or deconstruct both how we're telling our stories—negotiating the available discourses—and what we're saying. John Law argues that ephemeral, elusive, emotional, indistinct, and changeable experiences, like trauma, can only be known in embodied, deliberately imprecise, situated, allegorical, reflexive terms.[128] We *can't* "make sense" in any definitive way. Instead, we try to balance mystery with mastery.[129] We tell stories which are more or less real, or more or less useful, rather than offering tidy narratives with clear truths and morals. Such stories never really understand or enlighten, but, in theory anyway, they help us bear the unbearable.[130]

The issue of erasing alterity also pops up in relation to a third problem, which has to do with empathy. We often think of empathy as 'putting yourself in someone else's shoes.' But two people can't be in a pair of shoes at the same time. It implies displacement. Theodor Adorno says, when you believe you have mirrored the other, you have robbed them of their happiness, which is their ability to speak back to us.[131] Empathy is supposed to be nice, but it can also be "a dangerous act of enfolded cultural projection."[132] When we empathize with an other's story, we make sense of it in the context of our lives, often appropriating their story and hearing it only in terms of our own concerns.[133] As Tzvetan Todorov notes, "The illusion of fusion is sweet, but… its end is bitter, to recognize others as others permits loving them better."[134] Overwhelming or alienating otherness is a form of blasphemy.[135] It leads to much scholarly anxiety about the "violence of objectification" required to turn a life into a spectacle.[136] We may see empathy as a cure for objectification. However, as the feminist critiques of friendly research have noted, our feelings of warmth and communion are not guarantors of justice and respect.[137] Moreover, empathy may be beside the point, if the objective is not to communicate that discrimination hurts but rather that it is morally wrong and demands redress.[138] But *not* having empathy, *not* feeling with and for others and the othered aspects of ourselves, also seems unethical.

So what are we to do? Stephen Greenblatt describes a sense of wonder as "the decisive emotional and intellectual experience in the presence of radical difference."[139] Rather than empathize, Claudia Eppert asks us to withdraw from identification, from "imagining ourselves into the particularities of [others'] experiences."[140] Instead, we're asked to problematize our emotional and intellectual responses, to notice how they enable or obstruct our attentive engagement with otherness.

The fourth problem I want to raise concerns memory and forgetting. While the traumatized may be told that they must, literally and figuratively, "come to terms" with their history, they are also encouraged to forget.[141] This forgetfulness is vigorously promoted by those who are responsible for, or threatened by, our trauma.[142] Trauma narratives risk being received as old news—redundant, consumable, and relatively insignificant.[143] The over-exposure and misrepresentation of these stories inoculates us against their enormity and meaning. As Norman Denzin notes, "Anyone's personal troubles can now serve as a front-page story, couched as a banal morality tale with a happy ending."[144] Even public memorialization "can be a forgetting, a way of saying to survivors, … 'now you can put this behind you.'"[145] Minimization and forgetting are also common coping strategies.[146]

The process of testimony itself might paradoxically incline us to forget. In fact, that may be part of how it heals. Once a trauma memory becomes conscious narrative memory, a tellable story, the survivor may be able to change its meaning and move on.[147] This sets up a collision between our need for cohesion and closure, and our fear—both personal and social—that forgetting invites repetition.[148] This tension was described by Freud in terms of melancholy—with its chronic internalization and attachment to what has been lost—versus mourning.[149] The "right" choice, in most therapeutic frames, is mourning. However, it may involve "complicity with hegemonic assimilationist strategies."[150] It renders trauma as a personal, manageable, temporary set-back, rather than compelling evidence of enduring social problems, and enables us to forget. Some see this as "a sacrilege of the traumatic experience."[151] If our quest for social justice relies on our wounds, it may seem "virtuous to 'feed' righteous indignation, and treasonous to stop the rage."[152] Henry Krystal calls this a masochistic perversion that prolongs our suffering. We can't expect the wounded to stay bleeding in order to sustain a social revolution that may never come. But what should we do if the survivor mission that enables us to live with, and make sense of, our losses requires us never to heal?

The last problem with testimony that I want to bring up has to do with truth. Truth is a problem on a number of levels.

The first thing we generally want to know when we're told a story is whether or not it is true. However, if it's a trauma story, the question itself can seem vulgar.[153] By the 1990s some scholars had sacralized personal testimony as simple evidence to be affirmed and honored rather than interrogated and theorized.[154] The feminist literalist view argued that "women, whose experience of violence has been ignored, silenced, trivialized, and in general denied throughout history, must always be believed, *verbatim,* period."[155] In Freireian popular education models, stories were "unproblematically conceived of as suppressed knowledge." There was an assumption that the living voices or written texts of the oppressed "express a truth that will win out."[156] Unless, of course, those 'truths' were self-deprecating—in which case, they were seen as signs of internalized oppression, somehow without casting doubt on the general veracity of the testimony.[157] Language simply represented reality rather than constructing it.[158] Trauma survivors accessed painful, but irrefutable, truths,[159] and told these truths in order to heal.[160] The origin and organ of their authoritative knowing was a unified self, which could discern truth from falsehood through quasi-mystical means such as resonance.

Critics of this view—and there have been many—argue that we have no such self, and even if we did, it could not produce such truths. We readily resonate with lies or with representations that "reveal ourselves to ourselves as we like to think we are—a re-enchantment and depoliticization of experience and identity."[161] Our cultural obsession with authenticity, sincerity, true confessions, and sentimentality leads us to invoke 'personal truths' which are, according to Richard Schechner, "all too often a combination of clichés of intimacy, unexamined cultural fact, and romantic distortions."[162] What is happening inside my heart or gut or whatever well-spring of personal knowing I may claim is as subject to conventions and as socially structured as any other epistemology.[163] These relations of ruling are invisible to me and inescapable.[164] As Melissa Orlie notes, "There is a mystery at the heart of our being, a dependence that renders us fundamentally nonsovereign."[165]

The problem lies not in willful deceit, although that is always possible, but rather in the nature of memory. We assume the past is determinate, complete, and leaves a neutral, if somewhat inaccessible, archive in our minds.[166] However, memory is informed by ideological shifts, personal and historical events, and changing relations of power. Social institutions instruct us in what we should remember, what we must forget, how far back we should remember, how deeply to remember, and how to narrate the past.[167] Memory is thus a selective, complex, social construction.[168] Pamela Sugiman explains, "We remember what we need to remember, what is safe to remember, that which we have the cultural tools to express." Memory is shaped by our audience and our own "intellectual inquiries, personal needs, and moral imperatives."[169] We may be taught "to lie, or at least belie, ourselves as well as others."[170] As such, testimony given in good faith may simply reflect the prevailing discursive constraints and dominant narratives.[171]

Testimony may be better understood as a performative discursive practice. Performative utterances "make things happen rather than describing them.... They are judged by criteria of effectivity rather than accuracy."[172] Testimony cannot offer totalized, complete accounts. It is both formally and temporally complex, and may behave like fantasy.[173] Thus testimony can be "inaccurate, even flat-out wrong" without being invalid.[174]

This presents quite a challenge for scholars using testimony as a form of knowledge production. As Patty Kelly explains,

> The testimony of the survivor does not, in its articulation, determine meaning, and thus close a familial, cultural, or historical chapter. Rather the speaking of the trauma *opens* meaning, is productive of meaning, and necessitates a willingness on the part of the listener to bear witness to the catastrophic event, to untangle the narrative knots, and to listen through the gaps and ruptures, which takes precedence over any desire for finality.[175]

The challenge is not to adopt some ideal position of respectful skepticism, but rather to accept that the truthfulness of testimony may not be meaningfully adjudicable, and is probably not the most important measure of its value.

Are there any questions?

Metasophie: Can we go home now?

Scene Seven: People

Sophie is waiting for an elevator, calling home on her cell phone. She has a large knapsack on one shoulder and a bulky winter coat draped over her arm. Tahirih answers.

Tahirih: Hello?

Sophie: Hey, T. How was your day?

Tahirih: It was okay. Are you at school?

Sophie: Just finished teaching. Is Shawn there?

Tahirih: No. His car's gone.

Sophie: Okay.

Tahirih: How was your class?

Sophie: Oh, I gave a really long boring lecture on testimony.

Tahirih: *(laughs)* That's good.

Sophie: Yeah. I even tried not using big words, but—

Tahirih: I'm sure it wasn't *so* bad. Hey, I had this really weird dream last night.

Sophie: Yeah?

Tahirih: I remembered it at school. I was going to tell you about it.

Sophie: Mm hmm?

Tahirih: I forget. But it was *really weird.*

Sophie: Huh.

Tahirih: Oh, and Joe called.

Sophie: What did he want?

Tahirih: I dunno. He didn't say. You're supposed to call him back.

David—a mildly metrosexual professor roughly Sophie's age— approaches the elevators and smiles at her. He stands a few feet away. Sophie smiles and half turns away to finish her call.

Sophie: *(to Tahirih)* Okay. If Shawn comes in tell him I'm going to pick up supper on my way home. And remind the girls it's chore night, okay?

Tahirih: Okay. Bye. Hey, can I have a cookie?

Sophie: After chores.

Tahirih: Alright.

Sophie: Bye, T. *(hangs up, speaks to David)* Hey, there.

David: Hey yourself.

The elevator arrives and they both get on.

Sophie: Smoke break? I thought you quit.

David: Well, I did, but—

Sophie: I see.

David: How's it going?

Sophie: *(groans and shrugs)* Ugh. I don't know.

David: Excellent. *(smiles)*

Sophie: I have to start talking to people.

David: Oh, don't do that. People are annoying.

Sophie: They're scary.

David: Just do a theory piece.

Sophie: I know. But books only get you so far.

David: And you've got that *(waving his hand dismissively)* whole do-good thing going on.

Sophie: Yeah.

David: You've really got to get over that.

Sophie: I know. *(sighs)* People are so complicated. I have to deal with ethics and methods and power and subject positions.

David: I'm telling you. A nice literature review, you know—some analysis—

The elevator doors open. They exit into a network of tunnels.

Sophie: *(teasing)* I could be you.

David: Hey. My life is meaningless. *(smiles)* It's great.

Sophie: See ya.

David half-waves and turns, to exit outdoors. Sophie continues along the tunnel, passing between buildings.

Ubersophie: What was *that?*

Metasophie: Nothing. Get off her back.

Sophie enters a large empty women's washroom. She puts her knapsack on counter, sighs, and examines herself in the mirror.

Sophie: *(thinking, all at once)* I look like hell. Bad hair day. Angel had good hair. He said. Nice styles. Why say that? Is it true? Who cares. Pathetic. Vain. Pointless. *(Enters a stall, sits to pee. Continues thinking, while dialing Shawn's cell phone number.)* Did he pick up more insulation? Did he call about the dumpster? Did he haul the old hot water heater out of the basement? Did he get something out of the freezer? Did he take Ruth's project to school? Did he pee the dog? Did he talk to the electrician? Did he spend all day doing god knows what? Did he get any sleep? Did he get fired? Did he eat properly? Is David flirting with me? Did I do a good job? Is everything okay? *(rests her head in her hands while the phone is ringing, thinking again)* Did he take his bloody cell phone?

Shawn's Phone: Leave a message—

Sophie hangs up. Reaches into the dispenser for toilet paper. It is empty.

Sophie: Excellent.

Sophie puts her phone on top of the paper dispenser, digs in her pockets and finds a tissue. Stands and does up her pants, looking at her phone. She pauses, thinking, lips pressed together, while she puts on her coat and scarf.

Ubersophie: Oh, for God's sake, you're being ridiculous. Get it over with.

Sophie: I just don't have the *energy.*

Sophie zips up her coat, drops the phone into her pocket, washes her hands and scrunches her hair. She hefts her knapsack, looks at herself in the mirror, and takes a breath. A group of undergraduates enter the washroom. Sophie exits, back into the tunnel and outside. She takes out her phone and dials Joe's number, fishing in her pockets for gloves as she walks. It rings four times.

Metasophie: If he has something to say, he can call you back.

Joe: Hello?

Sophie: *(stopping in her tracks, clipped)* You called?

Act III
Asking Others

Scene One: Theory

Sophie is sitting in bed with Cricket, a small scruffy cream-colored dog.

Sophie: *(scratching Cricket's belly)* You're the only thing in my life that makes any sense.

Cricket looks at her thoughtfully.

Sophie: I don't want to do anything but lie in bed with the covers over my head. Just like you. All day. Why can't I do that, hey?

Cricket's back leg starts twitching.

Sophie: Oh, is that the spot? Yeah? D'you like that?

Sophie scratches vigorously and Cricket's leg jiggles. She opens her mouth and makes a long happy whine. Sophie stops scratching and buries her nose in Cricket's fur, talking into her belly.

Sophie: I don't want to get it wrong and then everyone will be disappointed and know what a stupid-head I am.

Cricket starts licking Sophie's face and nose. Then pauses, and looks at her seriously.

Cricket: You know that negative self-talk will get you nowhere.

Sophie: *(sighs)* You're right.

Cricket: I mean, I understand wanting external approval. You've seen what I'll do for a cookie. But why are *you* so worried? You're the alpha dog.

Sophie: Not everywhere.

Cricket: Whoa. *(pauses, considering)* Why not?

Sophie: Good question.

Cricket: But it still doesn't matter. *(sitting up, with her back feet splayed out and head cocked to one side, examining Sophie)* Let me ask you: how many women get abused by their partners?

Sophie: Well, that depends—

Cricket: Roughly speaking.

Sophie: About thirty percent?[176]

Cricket: And you don't think *any* of them have got something to teach you?

Sophie: Of course they do, but—

Cricket: "They?" Meaning?

Sophie: Survivors.

Cricket: That label signifies power relations, your willingness to identify with them, and your hope or cynicism about their capacity to change.[177]

Sophie: Well, what am I supposed to call them?

Cricket: Who said supposed to? I'm just saying. The terms are going to shape what you see.[178] And "survivors" sounds like some romantic TV show.

Sophie: You watch TV?

Cricket: *(shrugs)* The cats cheat too much for cards.

Sophie: Maybe I'm just opportunistic.

Cricket: You have to start somewhere. Perhaps you *are* playing off the cultural capital of working in the margins.[179] Does that make it bad?

Sophie: It doesn't make it good.

Cricket: Such black and white terms. *(shakes her head)* Have you thought about the ethics of doing research with 'sufferers' in general?[180] What that *means*?

Sophie: So, what—we *don't* make spaces for the suffering to speak outside of their own contexts?

Cricket: As if you could stop them. I'm just saying, be careful. Defining people in terms of their suffering has "profound intellectual and moral implications."[181]

Sophie: I also want to talk to service providers.

Cricket: Another awful term. Amazing that your language says anything at all.

Sophie: A lot of them are also survivors, but may or may not say so.

Cricket: *(nodding)* Professional consequences, I expect. Does it matter?

Sophie: I don't want to create a false dichotomy between them and the survivors.[182]

Cricket: But if you lump them all together…

Sophie: I'm not making authoritative truth claims anyhow.

Cricket: Isn't *that* convenient. Sorry. *(suddenly starts scratching her ear vigorously, then shakes her head, ears flapping)* The groomer didn't *(shakes head again)* pluck properly. Tickles. Sorry. *(pauses for a moment, collecting herself)* There are no perfect labels. As long as you flag their insufficiency, you should be fine.

Sophie: I'm also worried about subjectivities.

Cricket: In what way?

Sophie: Research reinforces a particular way of being a 'modern subject' and the colonial power relations that go along with it. But what if that's also the only kind of subject that fits "our common-sense understanding of (and commitment to) treating interviewees decently"?[183]

Cricket: Then you're ethically bound to an unethical

construction of subjectivity. You need to show that we build our selves and our lives based on our shifting positions in various discourses.[184]

Sophie: But we *experience* our lives as "personal, generally coherent, emotionally meaningful, narratively knowable, and tellable."[185] Where is agency if we don't have identity and can't represent ourselves?

Cricket: Whether or not you're a singular subject, there's plenty of agency available in reworking and resisting the way your subjectivity is constituted.[186]

Sophie: But we see ourselves as conscious, creative guarantors of meaning, not decentered actors.[187]

Cricket snorts.

Sophie: Are *all* dogs so postmodernist?

Cricket: Of course not. *(sniffs)* Mostly the French bloodlines. But you *must* focus. Have you considered Avery Gordon's "complex personhood"?

Sophie: She's so clever. *(sighs, scratching Cricket's head)* And she's right. People's lives *are* "simultaneously straightforward and full of enormously subtle meaning."[188] But what if *they* don't see it that way?

Cricket: To some extent you must use the modernist subject, if only because it's most familiar. You just have to bear in mind that it's a fiction with consequences. The lines around subjects are wobbly at best.[189]

Sophie: Sure. But I also need to respect the terms of others' identities.

Cricket: What about your own? Have you considered your position?

Sophie: *(gets a bag of knitting from beside the bed, and starts untangling various balls of earth-toned loosely spun wool)* Man, you made a mess of this.

Cricket: It was the cats. They're animals. *(smiles)*

Sophie gives her a look.

Cricket: And you're avoiding the question. Will you be playing the insider? The scholar? Or both?

Sophie: *(sighs)* That's tricky. I love how Lather and Smithies ask, "Who is this we/they?"[190]

Cricket: Posing as an outsider lets you insulate yourself and your readers, and makes you look less biased.

Sophie: Yes.

Cricket: But?

Sophie: I worry when I see a black scholar like Patricia Hill Collins calling black women "them,"[191] or when we ascribe all kinds of epistemic privilege to various marginal positions without being overt in claiming those positions for ourselves.

Cricket: But insider claims are also problematic.

Sophie: Well, insiders often can't just walk away with the data.[192] Your position might give you greater mobility or access to different discourses and communities. But being an insider isn't some sort of ethical insurance policy. It can also make you arrogant and blind you to really important issues.[193]

Cricket: Experience and identity don't equal critical awareness and understanding.[194]

Sophie: Right. And creating an "inside" can mean erasing internal diversity. Most of us always feel like outsiders anyhow.[195] I don't think I have delusions of being representative of survivors in any generalizable way.

Cricket: But it's also not honest to deny your investments.

Sophie: How do I know if I'm an imposter?

Cricket: You don't. *(sighs)* Just try not to appropriate or romanticize "the vision of the less powerful while claiming to see from their positions." Like Haraway says, "To see from below is neither easily learned nor unproblematic, even if 'we' naturally inhabit the great underground terrain of subjugated knowledges."[196]

Sophie: How can you *try* not to do something when it's the only way you know how to be?

Cricket: Remember that drawing inside-outside boundaries is a power move, not a move toward truth.[197]

Sophie: So all positions offer equal truth?

Cricket: What do you think?

Sophie: Nobody has complete or authoritative truth. But there is still more true and less true. Truths with varying outcomes or amounts of air-time.[198]

Cricket: So who's the expert?

Sophie: *(finishes winding her yarn, and starts knitting a slipper)* I want to say, survivors. We're supposed to see them as the absolute experts on their own experiences and needs.[199]

Cricket: Them?

Sophie: *(sighs)* She's the one who knows what's right for her, even if she thinks she's ignorant.[200]

Cricket: And she's the expert on the oppressor?[201]

Sophie: Right, the victim knows best. That knowing may be groping and uncertain, may be self-corrective, but it's still privileged.[202]

Cricket: But everyone can "claim to stand as oppressor and oppressed in relation to someone else."[203]

Sophie: And I don't know.... I don't think I necessarily know best about what's up with me. I *want* to see other women as authorities, as more reliable and insightful than the books. I want to trust them to know and explain what's happening in a useful, reliable way. I believe in the value of first-hand experience, and I don't think detached objectivity is ethical or possible. But we have different degrees of capacity and education, different amounts of self-perception or internalized oppression or magical thinking or whatever.

Cricket: Some of us have better noses.

Sophie: Maybe you can't adjudicate truth across discourses. But I also have problems with the idea of something being true-for-you. It's too atomized and relativist. I don't want kingdoms of one; I want a negotiated, complex account that respects community.

Cricket: You want all the truths to fit together like a quilt.

Sophie: Yeah. That would be awesome. If they all fit together. But of course they don't. We pretend they do, so stuff makes sense.

Cricket: Because you don't know how to think non-dichotomously.

Sophie: If the expert researcher is oppressive and bad, then the expert has got to be the participant, or intuition, or the body. Or the expert is nobody. But maybe we're all both experts *and* delusional. What you trust may not have much to do with what seems intellectually defensible anyhow.

Cricket: It's emotional, intuitive, instinctive. *(nudging a nest into the blankets by Sophie's leg, and curling up in it)*

Sophie: You believe what you need to be true.

Cricket: But of course the ability to make that truth stick depends on your power. And "power is presumed to equal oppressiveness."[204] So nobody wants to be caught being powerful.

Sophie: Right. The only ethical approach, for a feminist researcher, anyhow, is to minimize power differences. But of course we both have and want power.[205]

Cricket: Being wounded can make you even more interested in controlling others.[206]

Sophie: Which is really hard to deal with if controlling others is also part of how we define abuse. Maybe there's an important difference in the motivation or rationale behind it, but I worry that we're replicating harmful patterns.

Cricket: Even if you wanted to, you *can't* equalize power in a research relationship.[207]

Sophie: But there are more and less ethical ways of using it. It's not simple.

Cricket: Of course not. Because power is "capillary, nomadic, and circulating," not unidirectional.[208]

Sophie: The participants have their own priorities and goals, and I'm totally dependent on their willingness to play along. At the same time, this is my project. I take their voices and run with them.[209]

Cricket: Negotiating power or control over the data only works if both parties are interested.

Sophie: Right. And if an autonomous agent gives you her story and opinions, it seems a bit of an insult to turn that gift into me using my power to take something from her.

Cricket: You're denying the violence of objectification and appropriation?

Sophie: You're denying the possibility of non-exploitative generosity. They're not fools. They know research isn't friendship.

Cricket: Doesn't *that* solve a lot of your ethical problems. *(rolling over and writhing to scratch her back on the bed, then curling up again)*

Sophie: *(sighs)* It's a non-reciprocal process. But that doesn't mean it's inherently bad.[210] Trying to establish non-hierarchical research relationships means looking for a position outside the text—"a position that is politically irresponsible, empirically impossible, and epistemologically indefensible."[211] Ignoring my power is the surest way to misuse it.[212] I define the parameters of enlightenment.[213] I decide who to talk to, about what. When I write it up I use other people's words to make my points.

The best I can do is to make it really obvious that I am at the center of the text and that I don't know the answers.

Cricket: *(with a toothy, sly smile)* No worries there.

Sophie: Be nice. This is really hard. It means I have to make it personal.

Cricket: Ouch.

Sophie: I can't trot out my authentic story because I don't have one. But I do have to expose as much as I can of the "relations that influence the construction of the story that is told."[214]

Cricket: And most of those influential relations have to do with you?

Sophie: Exactly. And not just my intellectual life, either. So I'll have to borrow from autoethnography and write myself into the frame.

Cricket: Excellent.

Sophie: But I have to do *that* without upstaging the participants. Because really it's supposed to be about *them*.

Cricket: And, of course, they're all different.

Sophie: So I'll have to do one of those multiple-voiced performative partial truth things.

Cricket: A collective story?[215]

Sophie: Something like that. I can't trim and fit their stories into my paradigms,[216] but it's got to be cohesive enough to make sense. At least, kind of. It's got to be accessible.

Cricket: To whom?

Sophie: Well, ethically, to the people I work with. I don't want it to be one of those alienating, parasitic studies where people can't recognize themselves.[217] But it's also got to speak to other audiences. And get me a degree, so—

Cricket: They call it "difficult knowledge" for a reason.[218]

Sophie: No matter what, I'm speaking for others.[219] So I've gotta be careful.

Cricket: Lots of awful stuff gets done carefully.

Sophie: *(frustrated)* So what am I supposed to do, smarty-pants?

Cricket: You could just play.

Sophie: I am so not into that.

Cricket: You never take time to play.

Sophie: Come on. This is serious.

Cricket: It would get you out of your rut.[220]

Sophie: I'm in a rut?

Cricket: I'm just saying. It lets you see things differently.

Sophie: I am *not* in a rut.

Cricket: Have it your way.

Puts her chin on her paws. They sit in silence for awhile, as Sophie knits. Cricket falls asleep. After a few minutes, Sophie puts aside her knitting, curls up around Cricket, and pulls the blanket over both of them. Some time passes. Sophie wakes up sharply. Cricket is sitting on her chest, staring at her.

Cricket: So what are you going to ask your participants?

Sophie: *(sighs)* I don't know. I don't know what I'm seeing, how much I'm missing, or even how to locate those lacks.[221]

Cricket: That's good.

While they're talking, Sophie sits up and lifts the edge of the blanket. Cricket nudges her way under, settling against Sophie's flank. Sophie arranges the blankets so Cricket's head is poking out, and returns to her knitting.

Sophie: It's terrible. I'm totally incompetent.

Cricket: Not entirely. You can use the hunches, tensions, and disjunctions in your own life. Let it go from clarity to fuzziness. Your questions can change as you go along, and you might not see what was answered until you get to the end of it.[222]

Sophie: Please don't tell me to trust the process.

Cricket: *(laughing)* Okay. Don't trust the process. See how that goes.

Sophie: *(shaking her head)* My dog is a mindfulness meditation guru.

Cricket: What about methods? Have you considered cooperative inquiry?

Sophie: Hmm?

Cricket: You know. "Working with other people who have similar concerns and interests to yourself, in order to: (1) understand your world, make sense of your life and develop new and creative ways of looking at things; and (2) learn how to act to change things you may want to change and find out how to do things better."[223]

Sophie: Sounds good. And maybe something like feminist interviewing?

Cricket: But that's not easy, either. If trauma reveals the contingency of the social order, and how it conceals its own impossibility—who wants to hear that?[224]

Sophie: They'll put their best face on and try to give right answers. They'll follow the "culturally defined rules for appropriate behavior between strangers."[225]

Cricket: And so will you. And yet—

Sophie: I'll have to give up my desire for victory narratives.[226]

Cricket: Which can feel like giving up hope.

Sophie: Which is a lot to ask, when hope may be all that's keeping you going. How do you learn to hear what you don't want to hear, or can't hear?

Cricket: Of course a move toward the abject isn't always a move toward truth or reality. It isn't always helpful.

Sophie: Or possible. Even if I can find a way to say it, I have to trust that the witness can hear it without me having to take care of them and make it better for them. Where is that trust supposed to come from?[227]

Cricket: Have you noticed, with you, how many roads lead back to trust?

Sophie: Yeah.

Cricket: It's too bad you lost Molly. You were doing some good work.

Sophie: She may be completely right about everything, but she lost all credibility.

Cricket: Because her source of authority is a channeled intergalactic being named Abraham?

Sophie: *(laughs ruefully)* Call it epistemic differences. At least I still have you. *(pats Cricket)*

Cricket: That's a little ironic. *(shakes her head)* You're going to have to work on it. Before you can witness others, you've got to be able to witness yourself. You've got to deal with your resistance and fear.

Sophie: *(stops patting Cricket)* Oh, sure. I'll get right on that. And while I'm at it, I'll magically make space for answers beyond my intellectual horizon and emotional comfort zone.[228] Let people walk right in and destabilize me and wound me with their wounds.[229]

Cricket: You sound angry.

Sophie: How'm I supposed to *do* that? It's like saying, don't blink. If I'm not supposed to ask any questions I wouldn't be willing to answer myself then I might as well stay home.[230]

Cricket: Or open up.

Sophie: *(scoffs)* Like it's that easy.

Cricket: You could just holiday on other people's misery.[231]

Sophie: And call it a career? *(smiles)*

Cricket: So then the problem becomes guilt management.

Sophie: And nerves. You've got to seem relaxed and capable, or they'll think you're an idiot.[232]

Cricket: But you can't control your feelings, or theirs.

Sophie: *(sighs)* So you've got to open yourself up to sensory, emotional, and bodily life—all the stuff we usually suppress in our academic discourses.[233]

Cricket: Didn't I say? The anxiety could be a sign of potential, not pathology.[234]

Sophie: I've got to take in all of this *stuff* and let it affect and baffle and haunt me, make me uncomfortable, and take me down unexpected detours.[235]

Cricket: Is that contagion? Counter-transference? Vicarious trauma?

Sophie: No. It's about trying to be human.[236]

Cricket: *(snorts)* Is that the best you can do?

Sophie: If you don't listen deeply you only hear what you want or expect to hear.

Cricket: Which perpetuates colonization by reproducing dominant perspectives. But what do you hope to gain from that listening—absolution?

Sophie: No. The witness offers "fairness, compassion, and the willingness to share the guilty knowledge of what happens to people in extremity."[237] It's a non-interchangeable, sometimes involuntary responsibility.[238] You don't produce truth or meaning. All you can do is attend. You engage in a relationship of attention. *(sighs, looks up from her knitting at Cricket)* You make it look so *easy.*

Cricket: It isn't. "There is a risk, a stake, attention is not neutral, it is paid."[239] You've got to offer "an embodied cognizance" that opens you up and disturbs what it means to listen and learn.[240] Witnessing is an obligation, not a pleasure. It requires "an actual desire to go somewhere you may be hurt and stay there."[241]

Sophie: But you can't just take on some masochistic self-wounding shtick.

Cricket: Of course not. There's "an element of vitality, perhaps even joy, in the contact with another and the experience of being opened."[242] There's an ethical obligation to refuse despair.

Sophie: I guess I'm having trouble getting past the idea that my despair is unethical.

Cricket: It's just a little self-absorbed.

Sophie: Thanks.

Cricket: Being open to the other takes trust. You've got to quiet your ego, give it over to an intelligent and uncontrollable world, full of unimaginable potential. It's a surrender.

Sophie: I'm *working* on it.

Cricket: *(nuzzling Sophie)* I know.

Sophie: I don't *want—*

Cricket: You do and you don't. Hence your voyeuristic need to "find out" and comprehend.[243]

Sophie: So what do I do?

Cricket: *(shrugs)* What do you want to do?

Sophie: *(sighs)* Leave space for mystery?

Cricket: Or admit the space that's already there.

Sophie: Lash says "art has the capacity to leave this silence intact."[244] So I'll get my participants to draw or something, and we'll see.

Cricket: You can't just tack art on like that.

Sophie: What do you mean?

Cricket: Art is all about productive ambiguity.[245] Sure, it can represent messy experiences. But you can't just make it on purpose to help or solve problems.

Sophie: People do that all the time.

Cricket: People do all kinds of things. But art works by nonrational synthesis.[246]

Sophie: And scholarship is all about being rational.

Cricket: Right.

Sophie: So then what do I do?

Cricket: I suppose you'll find some manipulative pseudo-artistic compromise.

Sophie: Great.

Cricket: Your audience is much smarter than you are, you know. You don't need to change them.[247]

Sophie: But I've got to look like an expert.

Cricket: Aren't your participants the experts?

Sophie: Yes. No. We both are. I don't know. I don't want to change them, but I do want to help.

Cricket: You want to offer some kind of metaphoric fragmented thing where you're not spoon-feeding the reader fixed meanings.[248] Or, at least, not obviously.

Sophie: Yeah.

Cricket: But you also want to be a hero.

Sophie: No. Well, a tragic hero, maybe.

Cricket: Then you have three problems, don't you: how to connect with yourself, how to connect with their stories, and how to connect with them.

Sophie: Yeah. *(sighs)* It's all about the connection.

Cricket: No sitting on the sidelines, safe-distance cop-out.

Sophie: *(gloomily)* Yeah.

Cricket: Receiving what is there as nearly as possible, without evaluation or assessment.

Sophie: Yup.

Cricket: Not attempting to transform the world but allowing ourselves to be transformed.[249]

Sophie nods, sighs, and looks at her knitting.

Cricket: Existing in a state of mutual concern, caring and trust.[250] Feeling-with and receptivity. All that warm fuzzy feminist goodness.[251]

Sophie: *(muttering)* You needn't be so dismissive.

Cricket: Hey. I'm a *dog*. We *invented* the ethic of care.

Sophie: *(starts unpicking her work)* It all sounds so right, but something about it gives me hives.

Cricket: Distance is your survival strategy. You don't actually *want* to feel with anyone. At least, not in an unmanaged kind of way.

Sophie: Possibly.

Cricket: You don't have *time* for pain, yours or anyone else's. This whole *(makes air quotes with her paws)* "project" is really about avoidance. But the feminist theory you prefer requires you to remain emotionally connected and present.[252] So you're in a pickle.

Sophie: But principles don't magically make you empathic and non-manipulative.

Cricket: Try using them.

Sophie: A belief is not the same as a behavioral skill.

Cricket: So do something simplistic and shallow and call it feminist. All this angst is tedious. *(yawns)* Can we go out now?

Sophie: I know the right answer is to look at them, and me, with loving perception. Compassionate curiosity. Whatever.[253]

Cricket: The right answer is to keep asking questions.

Sophie: Just enough trust to initiate research, safe enough spaces for research relationships.[254]

Cricket: You'll do it wrong. Who cares. That's part of what makes it interesting.

Sophie: *I* care.

Cricket: I know, I know. We're working on that.

Sophie: How do I be respectful? I can't say they have false consciousness, because that implies I have true consciousness, but I also have to hear and analyze what they're not saying.[255]

Cricket: Yup. You middle class intellectuals still tend to see the disadvantaged as victims of distorted perceptions.[256] Like you're the only ones who really know what's going on. Participation becomes a token phase "in which all have their say in order to feel better before the expert tells them what they need."[257] If you assume you understand the structural causes of their problems better than they do, your "consciousness raising becomes indoctrination and domination."[258]

Sophie: But sometimes I think I *do* know better. Or at least differently.

Cricket: You *do* get the scholarships.

Sophie: And I can't just let their testimony speak for itself, either. I'm supposed to analyze it and deliver it to an audience and tell them what it all means.

Cricket: Yup.

Sophie: I've got to connect but not collapse differences.[259] Try to see from an other's point of view without imagining that it's possible.[260]

Cricket: "Loyalty to and identification with the fate of an other are not the same thing."[261] You can think you're trying to understand someone else's pain but end up making yourself the focus.

Sophie: I don't want to "other" these women.

Cricket: But you can't just identify with them, either. It gets in the way of actually hearing them, and it's too much of a burden on you.[262]

Sophie: So you want empathic unsettlement. Putting yourself in someone else's position without taking their place.[263]

Cricket: Assuming you understand and can participate in someone else's feelings about their experience "is, at the very least, condescending and insensitive."[264]

Sophie: But you always know how I feel. (*tousles Cricket's head*)

Cricket: *(smiles)* That's different. You could try something like Eppert's reading for alterity.[265]

Sophie: I've got to be receptive, passive and patient but not pretend to let participants run things.[266]

Cricket: Yup.

Sophie: I've got to bear witness to myself so I have space for the otherness of the other, but not get lost in myself and erase the other.

Cricket: It takes thinking. Opening up "a space of freedom in relation to what appears to be necessary."[267]

Sophie: I've got to get out there and try to make a difference in the world without presuming that I can actually *do* anything for anybody, or that they need something done for them, or that I've got something real to offer them.[268]

Cricket: Aiming to help suggests you are external and superior to the problem.[269] As soon as you assume the women need or want conscientization, you stop listening.[270]

Sophie: Assuming I was listening in the first place. It's not my best thing.

Cricket: Being trustworthy means you avoid "rescuing" others, even when asked, because this colludes in the suggestion that they can't act on their own behalf.[271]

Sophie: *(whining)* But *I* want to be rescued.

Cricket: That's clear. But you can't pretend you're going to save *them* with your healing power of art or truth or whatever you've got up your sleeve.[272]

Sophie: I've got to give up on certainty and use slow, uncertain, risky, troubling, vulnerable, quiet, diverse methods, but I also need to be able to explain and defend my findings.[273]

Cricket: Precisely.

Sophie: *(putting down her knitting, frustrated; she has unpicked the whole thing)* But I don't know how to do ANY of that.

Cricket: *(winks and smiles at her)* Sounds like you're ready to begin.

Scene Two: Practice

22 January 2008

I call the doctor to make an appointment. The receptionist asks what for. I say, "I think I am depressed." I have done the DASS diagnostic assessment, which found I was extremely severely depressed and extremely severely stressed. Afterwards I put my head down on my desk and cry. I feel so ashamed of being sad. I am so embarrassed that I cannot cope with life, even though "life" this week includes Shawn being fired because of his anxiety disorder, which renders him more or less incapable of completing tasks, which may render us more or less incapable of paying the mortgage. Dora is so emotionally volatile it is unbelievable. Tahirih is having full-on tantrum fits every other day. Ruth and Dora are both sick and so am I. My head is going to explode. I can manage one day at a time. Small bites.

To: sarah_todd@carleton.ca
29 January 2008

Hi Sarah—

I am working on the proposal, and it is a bit like trying to put back in order a few decks of cards that have been spilled on the floor, in the dark, with intermittent gusts of wind. There is so much that I could say, I am not sure when to stop (or even how to organize it in a really succinct way).

What I am wondering is how brilliant does this have to be? Is the aim simply to (a) show that I know something about the field and (b) that I have thought through my planned inquiry? Or is the proposal meant to showcase me, represent my best thinking, etc?

6 Feb

Feeling very lost. So much stuff did not make it into my proposal draft. So many dots I don't know how to connect. I am dropping so many of the things I need to carry. Feeling pretty discouraged about the whole thing. How am I going to make it all make sense? Still wishing I could read Joe's diary or speak to Angel, as if the facts might soothe me somehow. Like seeing a body so you can bury it.

11 Feb

The proposal is not brilliant, but at least now, with Sarah's input, I can feel the shape of it and know where it has to go. I wish I could write a lift-the-flap book. Or include photos and a fold-out tree of my intellectual genealogy. Or print the whole thing on paper made from the receipts for everything I purchased while writing it—all the cat litter and toothpaste and nails. Or hand-write marginalia and doodle all over the pages. Or write it like a make-a-mystery, where the reader has to choose their own ending. Would that be brave or stupid? Both?

22 Feb

I have a second draft for you.... this one was written with less ambient distraction (other than the freshly spayed, flea-ridden dog spastically flailing her cone-wrapped head around trying to get at her stitches).

I think it is better but I am sure you'll let me know…

4 March

I hate titles.
I am never any good at them.
I can write anything, but titles undo me.
I need a title for this dissertation.
I have spent the past half hour walking the dog all over town trying to come up with a good title. Now I have mud all over my kitchen floor and still no brilliant title.

27 March

None of this is urgent, so if you are in the grip of end-of-term madness, feel free to let it slide.

I have received feedback from the ethics office and made some edits accordingly.

I am waiting to hear back from the shelter—the director was away all this week, but I am to call her Monday. She'd like me to come in and meet with her and a couple other people in order to see if they can support my work or not.

31 March

Hiya

About the proposal defense…I have not really given it much thought, though I suppose perhaps I should. I've been too busy marking papers, installing joists and waiting for my interminable cold to end.

That being said, I have no familiarity with this sort of ritual and may be going into it with totally the wrong attitude. I am feeling pretty confident and hoping that all these clever people will offer encouragement and/or useful advice—I am assuming we are all on the same team and not seeing it as an inquisition. It seems to me that you are in charge, and if that is the case, I have no worries.

8 April

My proposal defense is tomorrow and I have no idea what is expected of me. Sarah says I should be ready to speak to the project off the top and then answer questions. I don't know what to say; I am feeling stupid and exhausted after four full days of working on the house. I just finished installing the bathroom subfloor today. And then became furious with Tahirih tonight. She was off the deep end because I was saying she had to finish her pork chop before eating a cookie and it went BAD. I was so angry because she was not listening and anyhow it was awful. And so now it is

9:30 and though I have baked the committee ginger cookies, I do not know if I have anything else to bring to this defense.

27 May

Is the ethics review ctee there to assess the rigor of my methods (my dissertation ctee's job, as I understand it) or to assess whether or not the methods will hurt anybody? It seems as though many of their questions pertain to evaluating the merits of my epistemology and methodology rather than determining the risks the inquiry might pose to others. Are they allowed to reject my inquiry, not because it is unethical, but because, for instance, they think autoethnography and arts-based inquiry are flakey?

24 July

We were supposed to be in by February and now we have one week to go. I have spent 14 to 18 hours a day at the house for the past two weeks—painting everything, scraping umpteen layers of toxic crud off the floors, sanding the original pine planks, and oiling them. Now it is really humid so the oil will not set and the floors are sticky and we still have to install the kitchen cupboards. We are $15K over budget—all on necessary things—which makes me want to vomit—and I have to buy a campus parking pass and four birthday presents this Friday, and I can't afford all the pretty things—the towel racks and curtain rods and all that stuff—which stinks. Nobody's going to say, ooo, look at that beautiful furnace. I am being a terrible parent—very irritable and intolerant—and that makes me want to curl up in a hole and quit. And my dissertation proposal is still in limbo waiting for the ethics ctee to decide if I can proceed or not. And Shawn's been sick since forever—a cold and now a flu on top of the general crappiness that goes with diabetes and sleep apnea etc. etc. The bickering never stops. (Him: you are always tidying up the shit I am working with and then I can't find it. Me: you never put away the shit you are working with and I also have jobs to do in this space. Repeat.)

And Tahirih is doing a summer course so she is not able to help with the kids or the house. And four nights a week I have to get all three girls at the same time to soccer fields in different parts of the county. And the ex-hole dramas never end. But most of all I am sick of being a person who dwells on what sucks.

6 Aug

I hope your summer is going well.…. school is probably the farthest thing from your mind but I have a quick question for you.

I have not heard back from the ethics ctee since they requested revisions (which I sent in on June 1). I have called and emailed several times. I am wondering if you think I ought to be doing anything other than waiting at this point, and if you know whether there is any compensation for students who can't do their work due to administrative delay (but pay full fees nonetheless)?

18 Aug

I have been trying to woo my brain into functioning for me so that I'll have at least thought things through before we meet tomorrow. I am feeling entirely discouraged (predictably, I suppose) and am hoping that I'll feel more optimistic about my dissertation after seeing you. I don't know what options I ought to be considering but I thought I should go back to basics and try to restate what my dissertation is all about.

This is what I said in my proposal: "This thesis moves into the gap between traumatic experience and representation, and asks how we render trauma communicable, if representing trauma makes sense of it, and whether sense-making is essential for recovery."

So far, so good. I am still on board with that.

However, I go on to say this: "It pursues these questions through participatory action, arts-based, and autoethnographic research in Lanark County, Ontario, in collaboration with survivors of spousal abuse. This research hopes to offer survivors and service providers creative recovery strategies, scholars deeper insight into the ethical and practical challenges of representation, and the host community education through activist performance." This is now seeming (a) really ambitious and (b) impossible to get through ethics review.

I don't know what their decision to send this to the psychology ethics review committee entails (or why—if that's who has to review it—it wasn't sent there sooner), but at minimum, it means more delay—which I can't afford. I seem unable to help them understand the line between PAR and therapy...the whole thing is really frustrating.

I think I'm going to have to cut the participatory arts based play-groups and ethnodrama and resubmit something which is (at least on the face of it) really conventional—which stinks, but so it goes. I can still do interesting things in the autoethnographic section (they don't seem to care if I treat myself unethically) and there will be other projects. To that end, I've come up with a few possibilities for us to mull over....
See you tomorrow!

19 Aug

How lovely to hold your baby and be able to talk through all my worries about my thesis. Thank you so much, Sarah, and don't worry about sidetracking into baby-land.... I think the world would be a much more civilized place if babies and children were more often present at so-called important meetings.

I have emailed the other ctee members with a brief heads-up on where things are going and how we propose to change my methods...I'll let you know what sort of feedback I get.

Thanks again and good luck with the sleeplessness.... I came home to find mine had all gone out cross-country running, but it feels like just last week they were spitting up all over my shoulder...

I also really appreciated you saying how you want me to love at least some part of my work.... that is really important for me to remember, as I am too prone to turning life into a series of hurdles.

1 Sept

I have not heard anything from ethics and am wondering how long I should let it slide before I storm in there and stand on a desk banging pot lids until somebody pays attention to me.... or perhaps another email would suffice?

17 Sept

So far this morning, Dora's window was left open all night long. Wide open. And the furnace is running. The kids took the garbage out last night—about 12 bags because I spent all weekend cleaning. I go to check on it at 7am and the truck has already been by and did not take a single bag because they did not put stickers on anything. So now I have to pick up the van at HB Auto, attach the trailer (currently full of scrap metal), figure out where to take it, empty the trailer, come back, fill the trailer, and take it to the dump, or I will have trash all over my driveway all week long. At twenty to eight I tell Tahirih she has to get going. At quarter to eight I tell her she has to get going. At ten to eight she comes down and asks for a drive because she is going to be late. I say no. She gets really sad because she expected me to say yes because IT IS HER BIRTHDAY and she thought I'd do it. And I am feeling DONE because I already made her a big fancy birthday supper last night and spent way too much money on her gifts and she's having a sushi party sleepover with five friends this weekend. But now I have to drive her or she'll be crying and late on her birthday. So I drive her. And then I come home and discover that someone has left the back door open. And, as I mentioned, the furnace is on. And whoever ran the dishwasher last night put it on rinse rather than wash so it all needs to be redone. Oh, and it's fucking meet the teacher night and Dora will be devastated if we don't go because there is some elaborate thing her class has arranged and Joe has decided that this week he is going to show up, so now I have to negotiate how to make it work and I don't want him going and showing off like he's so involved in his kids' lives when he doesn't even know who their teachers are. And Shawn is at a job interview for a government job that we really need him to get. So, no pressure. And now I just want to go back to bed but I started going to an exercise class last week and I have no excuse for not going and it is the only exercise I get and it is supposed to make me feel better but it just seems like another pain in my ass.

17 Sept

a bunch of little questions for you....

I've made a poster/flyer and am awaiting a call back from the shelter ED to hear if she minds me distributing it at Take Back the Night. I'll leave little stacks of them in likely places around town and put an ad in the local paper. I guess I'll give it a couple of weeks after I put out posters and if I have not gotten enough response I'll start beating the bushes a bit more aggressively. Does that sound right to you?

I was thinking about focus group locations. My parents have a big beautiful house nearby that will be empty a lot this fall (she's in NYC; he is in Baghdad).... Can you see a problem with having some of the focus group meetings there? It would make it logistically simpler.

I saw Andrea yesterday and she seems to feel things are on track and is going to send me a couple resources on feminist group interviewing. She was asking after you and baby and happy to hear that things had gone well.

I'll send ethics back the last change that they want but otherwise it seems like finally we're through those hoops. Sheesh, what a horror show.

I am also working on setting up a routine of some sort of arts-based research journaling or something—trying to come up with a semi-systematic reflective process that does not seem like an imposed hassle. I am concerned that if I don't establish my expectations for my own process nothing will happen—but that may be just my not-trusting-the-universe, control-freakish thing.

Hope all is well and that you're getting some sleep—

19 Sept

Well, I distributed some flyers and posters around town today and got my first call from an interested woman. She was really enthusiastic about it and is very interested in sharing her knowledge about recovery. Here's the problem: her dad abused her mom violently, but she says she has not been directly abused. The posters all say spousal abuse but I guess she feels like that includes her. I didn't feel like I could tell her no, you can't participate.... what do you think?

23 Sept

Restless and fitful sleep these past couple days since I started putting out posters for my research. I feel like a big fat fraud, like it is an insult to survivors for me to be claiming their subject position. Like I am going to get in trouble. I am scared about what would or will happen when Joe finds out about it. I was even scared to tell my mom about the autoethnographic part of my work—I could feel her concern about what havoc I might wreak with my irresponsible tendency to talk.

Shawn says I need to arrive at an understanding of why I feel like such an imposter. But even as he spoke in between us was a stirring or muted roaring, like an air conditioning or duct system—white noise. And a compression in my chest, like a coffee press slowly being plunged. And an immobility—curling in like a paralyzed hand. And I wish I could remember because it shows what I mean about the problems with testimony.

I've got too many voices in me. The only thing that makes sense is the dog sleeping with her head on my shoulder, under the covers.

26 Sept

Thanks for checking in.... so far my phone has not been ringing off the hook (or at all, other than that first day), which is kind of discouraging. I need to send out follow up emails to various folks and see what I can do.

On the plus side, I have a former student who used to work at one of the shelters in the city and who is very excited about my research and has offered to pull a group of suitable women out of her network and to host the group at her home in Ottawa.... I don't know if there is some problem with doing that but it sounds like a fine idea to me. So recruitment is not going brilliantly so far but it is still early days I suppose...

26 Sept

Getting the posters out has me feeling raw and gross and crazy and lost. So I had my kids pass them out at the Take Back the Night march when I should have done it myself.

30 Sept

Things are inching along...I have five service providers confirmed—a counselor, a doctor, a shelter staff person, a woman who runs the distress line, and a woman who works with victim services through the Ministry of the Attorney General—plus the woman who runs the sexual assault program out of the hospital has said she will send me at least one nurse who works on the front line with them. They aren't all available at the same time, of course, so scheduling might be tricky.

I am still talking to my contacts at the local shelter—I am assuming I will get at least a couple more from there. I have one survivor confirmed (yay!). The shelter folks also may allow me to go meet with their two writers groups and their assertiveness group—all survivors.

So things are proceeding...the ad comes out in the paper this Thursday so I may get some calls from that. It makes me feel so shy to ask people about it! But so it goes....

6 Oct

Spent the weekend blowing insulation into the attic. It's like tucking in blankets around the house's chin.

10 Oct

I know you are at your sister's and I hope the weather is as lovely in St. Catherine's as it is up here. It looks like a perfect weekend for studio tours and pumpkin pie and putting gardens and cottages to bed (which is what's on my agenda).

So far all the agencies I have contacted have been responsive and are sending someone (pending scheduling)—except I am having problems with the shelter. I think the situation is that my contact person there is a bit of a friend and wants to support it, but I suspect the new ED (who doesn't know me) is reluctant to get involved. I am still emailing back and forth trying to get them to talk about what their concerns are (so that I can have an opportunity to explain or adapt where possible). They are apparently going to talk about it again at their staff meeting next week but I don't have high hopes of anything being forthcoming. This stinks as they are the major gatekeeper to survivors and so far I have only one who has spontaneously called me. I am not feeling like the project is imperiled but it hurt my feelings that they weren't more open. So much for feminist solidarity :(

Anyhow, my former student has pulled a group together for me in the city…if needs be when I see them I will ask them all for referrals or ideas and maybe things will snowball from there. I just wish I had the data in hand so I could start working with it but these things take time, I guess. I am trying to be detached about the shelter issues—if they sign-on it is gravy but I have enough to go on either way.

I hope all is well with you and your little bundle of joy…

24 Oct

Well, I have a group here in town this Sunday afternoon, with five women confirmed, and I have another group next Saturday in Ottawa, and another one in Perth the following Wednesday. In addition I am doing an individual interview with a woman who can't make any of those meetings on Monday Nov. 3, and I have another willing participant yet to schedule….

so things appear to be chugging along at their own sluggish pace. I am feeling somewhat anxious about the meeting (it will be dumb, they'll all look at me like I am a moron, the recorder won't work, they won't want to be taped, the artsy fartsy activity will be lame, it will be awkward, the sky will fall)...all the typical thoughts. It feels a bit better if I pretend that this has nothing to do with school and it is just the same as the umpteen workshops I have done in gathering material for a play. The trick will be to somehow make it not feel formal (despite the huge consent letters and the recording device etc. etc.).

Luckily I have a whack of marking to plow through so I can't just fret myself into a tizzy.... although I would much rather be out walking the dog or planting my bulbs....

29 Oct

It went really well, I think. I finished transcribing it today—I am trying to stay on top of that, because I have other meetings Friday and Monday and Wednesday—and I also wanted to hear it all again while it was somewhat fresh.

There were four women. They all really engaged with the questions and the art activity and want to be involved in feedback/analysis reflection stuff through the website.... so that is all good. They were very positive and thanked me copiously for giving them the opportunity to reflect and participate in the conversation.... so all in all I think it went as well as could possibly be expected.

Anyhow, I think it was all because of the menu of snacks: brie and stoned wheat thins, nice hard black grapes, pistachios from the Middle Eastern grocery store, a poppy seed cake iced with chocolate ganache, and tea. We totally underestimate the importance of food in setting a mood, I think. Either that or I obsess over the food because it is the most readily controllable part of what is going to go on and my typical way of managing how people are feeling....

So the upshot is success! And I am quite proud of myself for having the thing transcribed already (the participants were incredulous that I was actually going to transcribe the whole thing…but if I don't how can they meaningfully engage with it, as it will already be so pre-filtered by me?).

The meeting this Friday has me a little scared because it is so many people in a space I've never seen (my former student's house!) so the logistics may be challenging—but there will also be a lot of enthusiasm, so I am sure interesting things will happen.

On going over the tape I did think of some things I would have liked to have probed further, so I may let my question list evolve, group to group. I don't know if I am going to be kicking myself for not being systematic enough, but going out there knowing exactly what I am hunting for seems like not what I'm into. As I keyed the meeting I bold-ed stuff that jumped out or seemed important for whatever reason—not trying to think too much yet about analysis. I am sort of hoping/trusting that if I just sit with all the data in my head and on paper, and listen into it, the stories it wants to tell me will come winding out. If not, I suppose I can still chop it up and impose some sort of order on it later.

Anyhow, I am now desperately late to get the kids to the Halloween fun fair at their school (and I still have one costume to make—yeegads!) so I am going to have to dash—but thank you for the email asking how it went…. I hope all is well with you?

30 Oct

I finished transcribing my first meeting. I really liked, actually, spending the time with the women again as I listened to their voices. I could remember their gestures, and how they looked as they spoke, and the movement of light in the room.

30 Oct

Thank you for your story about sleeping with your baby…. I miss the tactile and emotional intensity of those times. There is something so grounded about being close to an infant. My babies still come into bed every morning for a snuggle before getting ready for school and I am so glad that they do. Kids are awesome.

I will let you know how it goes tomorrow—today I am giving up on my lame attempt to mark papers and I will go shop and bake and do my ritual fussing….

I'm so glad you're my supervisor.

31 Oct

I don't know what, if anything, this will all mean in the end. But again the women were grateful to me for the opportunity, and seemed to trust that my work was meaningful and going to be helpful. One woman drove from two hours away for the meeting. They have so much faith in this, so much confidence. That is the trust they have placed in me: that I will do something useful. I am not sure how to do that but I will have to try.

I have not been keeping track, really, of who my participants are…although I guess my committee is going to want to know. I just hate how reductive those labels are…. it seems insulting to try and sort them by class/age/race/education level/occupation/years since they left their abuser/duration of therapy…. as if I could sum them up so easily. Most of the women I met today I know nothing about, though I suppose Dawn could fill me in if needs be. Of the seven women there, five made it clear that they had been abused by a partner, one said she had not been abused, and one did not indicate either way. Five of the seven have been or are service providers, in varying capacities—a front-line shelter worker, a provincial policy advisor, a counselor, etc. At the first meeting, two of the four women identified as having been abused, and the other two as having been through trauma, having had bad things happen to them, but not specifically as having been abused themselves. Three of them were service providers— in a social service agency, in a shelter, and in a private counseling practice. Of the seven women I've got coming up, two are openly survivors and six are service providers in the health/social services/justice system. This works out to eight women identifying only as service providers, four only as survivors, and six as both—but I am suspicious of tidy numbers like that.... what do they actually say about how credible or useful our conversations are? You can easily have been abused without self-identifying as a survivor, and many service providers can't or won't disclose. Even if they could be sorted into column A and column B, what does that prove? It's too close to the kind of power/authority moves I am working against. Even sorting them demographically gets messy.... I have one visible minority, one woman who said she's disabled, one with an indigenous background, two who indicated poverty...and a partridge in a pear tree. Just over half live in rural areas...they all seem to be 35–65 and heterosexual, and mostly middle-class. I know this matters because of the need for diversity and etc. etc. but I just can't find a way to think of them in this project in those terms. I can't ask when they left their abusers, or how much therapy they've had—maybe it would be rude and unethical or maybe I'm too shy. Even if I could map them ten different ways on a sociological grid, what would I actually know? They all got a poster or email or phone call, and drew themselves into the circle of people with something to offer.

I just didn't feel like I could ask them to justify their right to speak to the issues.

3 Nov

My interview went well today. Of course it got much more interesting after the tape stopped running, as I was standing up to leave, but so it goes. The woman is a psychiatrist who does a lot of work with trauma survivors.... so her perspective was very different from the others I have spoken with. It may be that through this research process I just get to the point where I start to figure out the questions I really want to be asking.... but that is to be expected, I suppose.

I didn't ask her to draw for me but it turns out she does art and singing and stuff as part of her own self-care/management of vicarious trauma routine. She also said I should let her know if there was anything else she could do for me, and if I was doing any arts-based projects.

5 Nov

I feel like I am blowing it by asking all these dumb questions and never really getting to the heart of what it is that I am really asking, the answers I really need, what really matters. I am afraid I am missing the point. That they are coming with a gift for me and I am never giving them the opportunity to give it. I am not attuned properly, or right-minded or grounded enough, I am too shy or inhibited or confused to see the simple question at the core of all this…whatever that may be. I am still imagining that this is a world of locks and keys.

Spent the day building a retaining wall and fence in the back yard.

15 Nov

Just had the last group meeting…

It was a different feel from other meetings—a third woman was supposed to attend but ended up being unable to do so (ex bailed on her kids). But the two who were there were therapist and (former) client…. which changed the dynamic. I also felt more comfortable with the women for some reason—maybe I am getting more relaxed with the groups, or maybe I am just in a different place.

I find it hard to do the art exercise because the things I want to draw I can't due to technical limitations. I also feel vaguely embarrassed because they create these ultimately hopeful things but my drawings are not hopeful. I feel like I have to make them hopeful in order to not worry people. I made my own image of the post-abuse process in two of the meetings…both times it felt awkward, as if I was making it about me or usurping the position of the participant.

It's freezing rain and raw and nasty and I've been transcribing interviews all day while waiting for delivery of the long-lost final kitchen cupboard fronts.

24 Nov

I hope all is well with you and yours…

I have spoken to 18 women now, with four group interviews and one solo. Each meeting took about 3.5 hours. I have transcribed them all, and am about to listen to them all again to go through and correct/revise the transcripts. I will be done with that process this week.

Shawn has started building the website for posting the transcripts and getting feedback—it should be up by mid December (I am hoping). I don't know how many of my participants will actually engage in the revision/comments process… I will be encouraging participants to not just edit for clarity or confidentiality but also to feel free to elaborate or add to what others have said—to add anything they didn't get the chance to say in our meetings.

My next step is to spend some time on reflective work—mulling the issues over in a non-linear way. As I went through the transcripts I kept thinking of follow-up question I wished I'd asked…. There's also possibly amateurish things I didn't do—like asking each participant where they worked or how old they were…. but I am sure I'll be able to make something out of what I've gotten. What that something will be, at this point, is a bit of a mystery…which may be a good sign, who knows.

9 Dec

Thirty seven years old today! Ruth and Dora have pinkeye—nothing like big green eye snots to start your day off right—I am working on organizing what I have heard and am now scrambling, because I've just been asked to teach a course starting in January (taking over from a prof who's gone off sick for the term). There's

200 students and 4 TAs and I have never done anything like it before so I am going to be all terrified by things like how to run the PowerPoint slides and what to wear and how to avoid being all sweaty and nervous...and I am still going to be keeping my TA position in Human Rights and writing the diss and raising three kids and keeping house...what could go wrong?

I am hating my mindfulness group—but they are helping me accept that I hate acceptance—not sure if that's progress or regression. Maybe I am just too cynical to get my groove on sitting there beaming lovingkindness out to the homeless people of the world and the whales in the ocean—or too churlish to follow a wannabe guru—or too invested in hopelessness. I can do meditative swimming or drawing or weeding.... I suppose it's a kind of illness when even your meditation has to be multi-tasking.

Endless hassles organizing the kids' Christmas schedules—but so it goes.

17 Dec

I know you are away but wanted to write this now so it gets out before my brain is consumed by other priorities...(it feels like I have an unruly pack of hyenas in my head competing for my attention as if it were some half-eaten antelope that can't possibly feed them all).

I have a question—which is not really a question, I guess—I have been coding my data—first by emergent themes, second by questions and their associated responses, and third by sticky phrases—things that just jumped out at me for whatever reason. My fourth sort was going to be just by visual images—working into a visual analysis using their artwork—perhaps with me creating a composite visual piece that combines and borrows from the images they created (via scanning/cutting/pasting etc.) and connects the visuals with a hybrid of the narratives they used to "explain" their art. I don't know if a collective image(s) will emerge but it seemed like it was worth pursuing as a mode of analysis.

On my way there, however, I stumbled into another strategy.

Laurel Richardson is offering a workshop at this year's Congress of Qualitative Inquiry, in which participants have to write a piece that is both personal and historical (sociological) using only three word sentences. I was mulling over the point of this exercise (other than fun) and it occurred to me that maybe I could adapt it as a verse-form method of analysis and presentation. What I like about writing poetry is the close to the bone feeling that comes when language is stripped down and spare—and I felt like my data was buried in words. So mostly as an experiment, I've gone through and condensed the transcripts—keeping the images, the issues and opinions (more or less) intact. It's a bit like looking at a sine wave and keeping all the peaks—the places where their voices advance or reveal, like bright spots on the page—where the motor of reading slows down to work through a thick chunk. I'm keeping the distinctive turns of phrase—lines packed with personality—but sifting out all the extraneous text—including who said what. I'm a bit worried about it (what if this unethically erases authorship, diversity, etc.) but given that their voices are mediated by me anyhow—and the point is what they're saying, not who is saying it—I thought it might be okay or at least interesting.

Rewriting all the group interview transcripts in (more or less) three word lines has allowed me to really see the shape of the data, almost like lines of melody. I'll leave a few stories intact—longer bits where we hear one voice, like an aria or solo passage—but most of it will get chopped up (literally, with scissors—my brain can't do this on-screen). I'll sort and tape them back together, clustered around themes and tensions, to see what lines emerge. I'm hoping that, by organizing it thematically, I'll be able to combine voices to call out the tensions and harmonies and produce a sort of analysis by juxtaposition, like a piece of choral music. It's a way less didactic approach than "proper" analysis but maybe it'll move toward that slower, more humble, exploratory sort of knowing that Lather and Law are reaching for.

I've sung in a lot of choirs and there is this amazing thing that happens when you are singing full voice but so well attuned and arranged that instead of hearing yourself you hear some-thing far bigger and richer and more complicated. I don't know if I can do it but it would be great if the participants got a bit of that feeling from the way I made their voices sing.

My worry is, to a reader, it could look like I've just dumped some semi-processed data disguised as lame free-verse poetry...
it takes some patience to put up with not being told what stuff means (it's a lot easier to be pomo in theory than practice) and the form might seem deceptively simple. They could also feel flooded—but that is what trauma does, I suppose. What do you think? Is this a legit method of analysis or just me being freaky?

Hope you are having a wonderful time at your sister's place...

30 Dec

Shawn got laid off today from his hardware store job, which is depressing. There were no customers the whole Christmas sea-son, so no real surprise. And all the deferred reno bills are com-ing due. Also a tree blew down in the backyard this morning. It doesn't look like it did much damage but it did hit the house and we've not been up on the roof yet to check. At minimum there's a honking big tree to chop up and haul away. So far we have not been hit by a plague of locusts so at least there's something to look forward to.

6 Jan

Happy new year to you, too! I was going to email you tomor-row, actually, as I am hoping to have the last bit of coding done by the end of the day and was planning to crow about it. I am a little worried about how I'll find some threads or patterns or meaning...how I will decide what stories the data is telling. It's not like putting together a puzzle or comparing apples and oranges—more like apples and lawnmowers. I am trying not to worry about it though...my brain seems to be a pattern-finding (or creating) machine and I am hoping that all I have to do is pay attention to what I am doing involuntarily. It's like an artist, I guess…the challenge is not the seeing, but rather allowing what you see to be how it is, rather than what you were expecting or hoping to see. I also have to get around my irrational anxiety that someone is going to tell me I have done it all wrong. I am not used to being the expert on my own project and I guess I am still looking for the approval of a Big Other (go figure). But I am trying not to go too far down that rabbit hole because I know if I actually do produce something ridiculous or inappropriate or weak or whatever, you won't let me go out there with it into the critical world and get creamed. I am probably more likely to weaken my work through excess timidity than excess boldness, and I suppose even being spectacularly wrong is not necessarily a waste of time. All kinds of idiocy gets published and funded. I just need to have faith that my form of idiocy is worth writing.

I did take some time off at Christmas to do rolled cookies and grandparents and all that stuff…with an undercurrent of anxiety, of course, but I think nothing short of a lobotomy would change that. Having been away from my participants' voices for a bit I am finding my emotional response to the material has changed—I find it more difficult or depressing to fill my head up with abuse when I haven't been thinking about it for awhile. So I take breaks. But I am really trying to push through it, because I think the longer you spend out of it the harder it is to get back in.

Maybe I will come by for tea sometime when I have been beating my head against the data for a few weeks and it still isn't speaking to me….

Thanks for checking in.

9 Jan

Stopping work early to build a fort with the girls when they get home from school in the enormous pile of snow I shoveled out of the driveway yesterday, hoping it will distract them from the burst of sorrow they'll feel when they come in the door with their toques on crooked and I have to tell them that their dad isn't coming to get them this weekend (again).

20 Jan

One of my students is angry because I wouldn't let her switch into a group with her friends. Now she's claiming I said Muslims are assholes, immigrants were welfare bums, that I'm condescending and biased, etc. etc. She is pursuing formal charges of discrimination!!! Now I have to record EVERYTHING to protect myself against further allegations. At least other students have vouched for me—so it's a major pain in the ass but I shouldn't be in any danger. It's a good lesson in boundaries—the whole world is not going to love me and that's got to be okay.

8 March

Things are going alright…

I have not been able to do much on the dissertation as I have been (not so patiently) waiting for Shawn to get the site on line and the password protection sorted out so my participants have a chance to look at what I've done securely before I get totally invested in it as is…but the site is now up—you can check it out if you like—www.sophie.tamas.com.

It's looking like I may not be able to integrate everyone's visual work into the final text, and color printing may be a problem…if so, I could create a gallery of images on the website…what do you think?

13 March

The kids are home for the next nine days on March Break. They are going to want to do really annoying things like speak and walk around and make noise and I will feel guilty for not doing fun stuff with them and working instead. Or perhaps jealous…

2 April

I am rereading my thesis proposal and noticing the big differences between what I proposed and what I have done. In my dissertation, do I need to speak to (explain, justify) these discrepancies? Or is that something that I would do orally, in my defense? Are those discrepancies okay?

In terms of where I am at with the project, I am coming to the end of gathering ingredients. I have just finished going through all of my database of notes, and pulling out about 250 pages of potentially useful/relevant quotes—as a sort of thematically organized bank of other peoples' pertinent ideas. I have also reread most of the papers I've written in the past few years, and noted bits that might be useful or relevant.

I am currently compiling my own journal entries related to the dissertation that I have been keeping (off and on) for the past couple years, and getting those thoughts organized. I have not heard much back from the participants about the data—but I don't want to pester them for reassurance.

Next I am going to spend some time with my interview findings, seeing how or if they connect with all the other material I've got on the table. I've really enjoyed working in verse form.... I've organized the findings around the themes that emerged from the women's voices and used spatial arrangement on the page to show the tensions and overlaps. You can't always tell when the words move from woman to woman and often several voices are combined in one phrase or segment. I've done a little grammatical smoothing (verb tense, etc.) to make it flow but otherwise it's all their words.

Creating it was a lot like writing counterpoint, but I am not sure how to help the reader receive it as a piece of choral music. I could use musical terms—andante, con bravura, con amore, doloroso—all these delicious flags for emotionally shaping a performance—but I am afraid that would be like back-seat driving—too prescriptive. Sub-headings may not be much better, but the reader will need some kind of navigational aids, to show the compositional logic. I feel like I have worked the material over pretty heavily in getting it onto the page—there's a lot of analysis embedded in how it's presented. I don't want to chop it up and feed the reader one pre-digested bite at a time...of course it's all how I heard them but I really want some space for us to just *listen*—which isn't easy. To read text like music.

I am also not sure how I'll integrate the findings into the dissertation.... really, they need to be at its heart. I am worried that there's too much me.... but I suppose hearts are, relative to the body, quite small and off to one side. I just need to clearly show that the findings are what make the whole dissertation live, they're the underlying pulse, circulating through everything. I've thought of extending the musical metaphor to frame the whole diss as a sonata—with an introduction, first movement exposition, second movement development, third movement resolution, and final coda—but (a) that could easily come across as too high-culture/elitist, (b) I know nothing about sonatas and (c) my brain is more likely to think in acts and scenes.

My plan is to have an outline for the dissertation roughed out by the end of this coming week. To me, outlining is really the creative part of the project, so I am hoping my brain will be ready. I will have to make some important decisions about boundaries, mandate and form—balancing what I want to do, what I can do, and what my audience will accept. This could end up being the kind of writing I *can't* outline...so we'll see how that goes.

Next week will be eaten up by marking exams, but my plan is to start writing on Monday April 20. I am presenting at two conferences in late May and going to a week-long Gender and Health research thing out west in June, but I am hoping to have something like a good draft together before the kids are out of school.

Thanks again for all your support,

Sophie

4 April

Dream that I have been asked to join a small choral ensemble. I tell the conductor I don't think I am ready for it, that my voice is not strong enough, and she says she thinks I will do fine. There are only two altos. We start practicing but instead of sheet music I have a book of poems. I can't find the page we are singing from. Everyone else seems to know what to do. Are they improvising? It feels good to be in a choir again. I have forgotten how much I miss singing. I try to join in, to copy the other alto, but I am not doing it right. Then I am told there are two alto parts, so we have to sing different lines. The other alto is trying to help me find my place, but our books are different. Are you ready? the conductor asks. Yes, I say, but I am not.

ACT IV
Findings

Scene One: Poems of Others

Sophie's dissertation defense, in a large seminar room. The committee sits behind a long table, facing a wall of windows looking out over fields. Sophie enters, and stands in the middle of the room.

Sophie: I am not sure how to begin to represent my dissertation. Sarah said I should summarize it, and speak to its tensions, problems and possibilities. But how do you summarize a project of unknowing without being unfaithful to your own theoretical framework?

A zipper pull appears between her teeth. She grasps it and pulls it down, unzipping herself to the waist. The participants step out of her chest: Margo, Olive, Alice, Stella, Dawn, Ubah, Tammy, Victoria, Belinda, Cheryl, Heather, Dr. White, Shirley, Anne, Anna, Alexa, Jen and June. They appear simplified and flicker a little, like ghosts. They form a semi-circle, facing the committee.

Sophie: *(to the participants)* Thank you. Thank you all, so much, for coming. *(zips herself back up again, turns to the committee)* This is how, or if, we recover.

Sophie faces the women, both hands up, like a conductor signaling a choir to prepare. She makes eye contact with each of them, nods, and they inhale together into the opening bar.

RECOVERY

Do we recover?

(yes)

Definitely yes
healing is possible
it's amazing what
happens sometimes
without a lot
of intervention.

I have seen
amazing resilience
and I trust
that it's there.

The human spirit
just has this
drive for life.
People find a way.
It's a mystery
to me where
that comes from
but I see it.

(maybe)

It's not quick
so many factors
in optimum circumstances
over time yes
recovery is possible.

I'm not going
to let him win.
After sixteen years
I'm whole again
I'm almost there.

I don't think
we've discovered yet
really good ways
of transforming
ourselves beyond
but I want
to believe that
it's possible.

(no)

Sometimes you never
recover from traumas.
Recovery almost has
a cruel sound to me.
I don't expect it.

It's been fourteen
years. I will
never recover.
I acknowledge it.
It's always there.

It takes part
of your fundamental
being away. You're
always looking to
recover that part,
always changed.
Can you heal?
No.

(yes)

I'm amazed at
the spirit in
women who leave
who make a new
life for themselves
sometimes with few
resources. Hope is
very key in
people's ability
to carry on.

They keep going.
They manage. They cope.

It doesn't haunt
me. I don't
think everyone
loses themselves.
A little part
of you knows
it's not right.
I hung on to that.
That was my tree.
We're all dealt
something in life.
I can be
who I am.
You have to
believe in yourself.

(maybe)

I like the idea
that people recover
but like chronic illness
you don't necessarily.
Illness and health
are not opposites.
You achieve
wellness, maybe.
It doesn't disrupt
like it did.

I don't mean
they go well
but, by golly,
they do keep going.

Like broken bone
you get treated
after some help
the pain goes
you always remember
under an x-ray
you see the crack
but things are
alright for awhile.
It might come
back like arthritis.
You have to
take care of yourself.

(no)

It's so
traumatic you can't.
You survive because
you have to.
To lay down
and die, no.
It doesn't go
away. There's no
magic. People carry
their wounds forever

often in a great
deal of pain,
using some crutches.

The dream you had
family you hoped for
part of you
you can't get back—
there is a
kind of death
that's happened to you.
People who come
to a shelter,
they've died.
You separate inside
to get things done.
You don't heal
like broken bone.

Do partners help?

What helped me
was a partner.

I was in a
quite suicidal place
just given up.
Actually finding love
hope in another
person's eyes
who absolutely believed.

You're not alone
suffering will end
you will trust yourself
in stages, eventually.

I'm at the point
fuck the relationships.

I've learned but
I can't say
who I'll pick next.
I can sense smell
feel who's going
to beat me
financially break me.

They're bad for me.
I'm attracted to that.
I can't trust
that part of me.

I never had
another relationship.

I'd always be watching
if he raised
his hand to
scratch his head
I'd be like
you are going
to hit me, go.

You lose trust
in your ability
to see. It
sneaks up on you.

Where do we get stuck?

We're creatures
of habit, you know?
I still go to
the wrong cupboard
for the coffee,
the places that
things aren't there.
I'm thinking I'm
in my house.
Then I correct myself:
I am at home.
    That's very hard.
    Home is huge,
    your safety net,
    all you know.
    Suddenly you're gone.
Part of you
is always connected.
All the memories
can be dangerous.
It's easy to fall
into depressions.
You have to learn
like baby steps.
That was then,
this is now.
    Go to that
    happy place.

The longer it's
been, the longer
it takes.
    A song, a smell
    a season will
    take you back.

You can't help it
my brain a bunch of doors
one opens up
and I'm shaking.

I thought I was
so strong, moved on
then something hits you
boom right in your face.

Your kids are
a constant reminder.
    To break up
    my son't home
    the guilt pretty near
    ate me alive.

The other fish
the fish that's hooked
looks crazy, right?
But that fish
is working for its life.

Like a rogue virus
that jumps in
and takes over.

If I forget it
might repeat but
my happiness depends
on whether or not
I can forget.

I never will be
that's part of me
and I don't really
want to say, okay
I'm recovered, goodbye.

The aftermath doesn't
go away.

You see little things
and don't recognize them.
I tried to get
out of my first
date with him.
He just absolutely refused.
That annoyed me a little bit.
It used to be the joke.
Or one time
he fell down
the basement steps
only a few steps
but he punched
a hole in the wall
he was so angry.

He was never
one to physically hurt you
he'd go on rampages
which was worse
slamming the cupboards,
the doors.
Disrespect for property.
You think, oh,
he's got a bad temper.
He's an Irishman.

Well, we don't come
with instructions, hey?
No one comes with instructions.

I keep thinking
I see my mother in law.
She died during the separation.
She was good to me,
you know
and I didn't have a chance
to say goodbye to her.

Every once in a while
I'll see this
little old lady
I'll think it's her.
It's the strangest thing.
She had a hard life.
I can understand
what made her
the woman she was.

They were always
gruff with mom
a lack of respect
toward their mother.
She was this
kind little old lady
would do anything
for these kids.
Baking, cooking, you know.
She'd put up with them
being ignorant with her
and you'd think, wow.

She left in the end
after 38 years of marriage
she found her courage.
I could understand her fear
of not having her children around.
She knew.
She knew.
But I understand, now.

In your life
you're traveling from
spot to spot
in your mind
you're all over the
place.

All that weight
carrying that guilt
locked up like a
bottle.
You can't become
the person you are.

There's days when
I feel like a hero
like Superwoman.

When you walk
out of that marriage
that's a battle.
That's a big one.

You're dying
so suppressed
so unaware of your
needs wants
desires dreams.

You still
go back there
every once
in a while.

I done this.
Let's see
what else I can do.

How?

People find all
kinds of ways
of expressing trauma
  pre verbal, sub verbal
  outside the realm
  of your world
creative processes   words enacting art poetry drawing journaling music play
  come in, tapping
  your inner guide
    (who?)

  like you were
  back, really back
  as a girl.

Best of all worlds
telling helps a lot
takes a lot
to do it, though.

One wrote əsnqɐ
upside down

      cannot deal
      with that word.

111

Why?

It's important necessary
had to divulge
verbalise on some
level tell
their story
stored like luggage.

Telling oneself
can be the
hardest part.
You talk, you
think, things
come out that
you didn't really—
you know.

(to know yourself)

What the connection
is between play
and thinking well
of yourself I'm
not sure but
it's important.

They start to paint.
There's a purity
and humour in that.
The rest of the
world go hang.
In the moment
you can't go wrong.

(you're safe)

Talking helps process emotions
put in perspective
make sense, categorize.

I found a counselor
in the yellow pages
spilled my guts
and said, okay
I need to know.
Was it?
Am I?
Am I being a crybaby?
She just looks at me.
She says, yeah.
You were. Really. Yeah.
That whole weight went off.
You think you're going crazy.

(validation)

You talk and
talk and talk.

At the gym
strangers ask
how you're doing
and it all starts
coming out.

After I said
I didn't mean to,
sorry. And they
said it's okay.
I've been through
the same.
You start
forming connections.

(connection)

You feel compelled
to talk, testify, tell
what happened to
you.

We all want
it better for
the next woman,

to make a difference
to someone else.

(your mission)

112

Why not?

They may very much
regret telling because
it changed their whole lives.

Police are required
to lay charges
victims are required
to tell and again and again
and all of a sudden
she has no money
he's after the children
he's set a trial date
he gets away with it
he gets off.

She's worse off
than she started.

(fear)

You may say
you didn't let
it get out of hand.
It wasn't so bad,
no big deal.
You blew it off.

It feels worse

to deal   to think
with that   I was
terrible   at one time
feeling.   helpless.

(minimizing)

You may be silenced
disbelieved
discounted
told it doesn't matter
get on with your life.

It may be
used against you
you're just
hurt again.

Everything you
had to say is
under the carpet.

We don't want you
to talk about it.

(suppression)

113

Women from certain
cultures will be
believed because
you know,
        those men.

But if he is
mainstream why
wouldn't you want
to be married to him?

If you regained
meek, broken down
you may be believed.

If you regained
your power,
you're very vocal
asking for support
you don't look
like an abused woman.

(stereotypes)

When you talk
about it you
        can't move
                past it

        relive it
        over and over

open that door
digging things out

                constantly justifying.
I've done enough.
I'm tired.

I don't want
to deal with
it anymore.

(justifying)

The sorrow, the sorrow
the hurt, the hurt
the pain, the pain
        when it identifies
        who you become
        you're very lost.

I hope to
learn from it
but continuing to talk
brings me back.

It was horrendous.
It was done.

Like being naked,
there's a limit.

(naming)

I don't want to be remembered
as a "survivor."

I've never looked at it
as "surviving."

I'm not a
major survivor
but I think we've all had
something in our lives.

Survivor is a good word,
a strong word
but one woman hated it.
        She said,
        I'm a thriver.

                                    Recovery sounds
I must be naïve   like I am
I never thought   recovering from
of it as   alcohol and
"recovery."   drug abuse.

I understand   It sounds like
now. I do.   it was your fault.

Some never tell.

114

DUET: TAMMY & DAWN

When you hit
rock bottom crash
you need someone to
watch over you.
I had my parents, my family.
I remember like
it was yesterday.
I had my son
who was three
I packed everything
in the car
and took off.

My parent's home
I was raised in
was always a safe place.
The minute I
stepped onto
their property
the minute my feet
touched that grass
I felt my body
start to burn.

I had no period.
I was 107 pounds.
I had nothing left in me.

I went through
the motions
son bath snack bed
before my head
hit the pillow
I was out.

Being able to
feel from
the neck down
is really hard
in this process
for me.

Being angry.
I'm not able yet
so I guess
I'm having a
hard time
getting it out.

For me it's not
recovery of
who I was
because
too many things
started happening
right away.

You're broken.
Your spirit is
broken,
you body is broken,
your soul.

You need someone
to put their
energy around you
and say, *you're safe.*

I can do
self-compassion
for other women
but it's very
very hard
to do it
for myself.

Once you've got that
you can't do everything
but you can start to
survive
little by little.

115

Personal Characteristics

Financial. That's how
they control.
You've got to
be able to
take your losses.
There's nothing
of value if
you're dying inside.
Run with a bag
if you have to
        but that's not
            for everyone.

(grit)

I allowed someone
else to control me.
I used to look
in the mirror
and think, ugh!
Now I don't
see that person.
I like who I am.
I'm vibrant, happy
in control of my life
and my destiny.

(control)

One of the most
inspiring things
is the courage, the spirit
that will not lie down.

A lot of women
don't even have
the courage to say
hey, I need help.
Women don't.

If you reach
out for help
and don't get it
where is the courage
to do it again?

We don't look in
until we move on
look at ourselves
and say, wow.
I had the courage.

(courage)

You make time
to look at it
an internal commitment
it's a lot of work
to do that so
some just aren't willing.

Some take medication
in hopes that they
don't have to
look at it.
Which is fine.
Their choice.
Healing is relative.

You can take that
and carry on
or let it make you stop
if you don't work
to get better.

You have those choices.
Sometimes you do.

(will)

So many women
come in black and blue.
How they recover?
At some point they
must want to
let that go.

Sometimes people
are ready to work.
        Sometimes they're
        not as ready.

I'm healing because
I want to heal.
I want to move on.
It's made me much wiser.

Not everybody is into that.
Not everybody wants to.
It's not the right time,
or whatever.

Sometimes things
immobilize us
until we tap
into that thing
that makes us strong.

Recognize where
your strengths are,
where you need to grow,
to find connections.

When you start to heal
all that repairs itself
if you can recover
the strength and courage
to say, this is how
you make me feel,
to leave.

        Wome who
        get strong enough to leave
        give me hope.

(strength)

117

Intangible Things

You need time, often.
Very traumatized people
it takes them years.

(time)

You need to
know your choices
trust yourself
be taught how
to make decisions
because that whole
step has been
taken away.

(self-trust)

Sometimes you have
to rip everything down
that terrible nothingness
until you can
rebuild again.

Your identity is lost
who you were
who you are
you have to
find yourself.

Women reinvent themselves
change their given name
cut their hair
get tattoos or piercings
silly as that sounds.

You've got to
have a self
then you work
on the esteem part.

(identity)

You should
put his name down
on school forms
not argue with
the teacher

go here
say this
act this way
do that

follow the norms
a certain way
you're supposed to
or else.

Your insides
are enraged.
You want to
be respected.

You're so vulnerable
no should do-ers.
I was always
doing it wrong.

(respect)

For years
all I wanted was
to be truly hugged
by someone who loved me.
It was just
something I craved.
Had to be
the craziest thing.

Back home I had
my grandma, my aunts
around the corner
Now I don't.

I got to the
point where I
didn't have anyone.
I'd already hidden
what was going on.
You're by yourself.
How do you
face people?
What do you say?

You should have
someone to sit
with you when
you're scared.

someone to listen
to your secrets
and say, you're okay.
It's not your fault.

someone who's going
to let you cry
let you get angry
and say, you'll
get through it.
Just make it to
the end of the day.
Hopefully, tomorrow
will take care of itself.

that strong
friend who can
speak for you,
go to the doctor's,
have a cup of coffee.

someone to call
and they come
and get you.

I don't want to
look at a man
deal with a man
a man doctor
a man officer
a man anything.
I need to talk to a woman.

(care)

119

Tangible Things

What women need
is to be able
to use a gun

is to be
medically cleared
literally stitched up.

is a sandwich
and a cup of tea.
Cereal for the kids.
If we make
the kids happy
the woman will stay.

Chocolate is a really
important part of recovery.

is to change
the environment.
Remove yourself
no matter how hard.
Change something.
Not everyone can.

We have a
really good protocol
constantly under scrutiny
by all of us
to ensure the support
networks are there,
in the community.

As long as
they want help
we can provide
it for them
with all the
community partners
police, crown attorney
family lawyers, counselors
probation officers
Interval House
some monies for
lock changes
although that
could be improved.

People want
to feel safe
first and foremost.

They come for
safe haven first
and sometimes
we send them
right back out
with no safety net.

120

The first thing
you need is
a place to live,
money, financial assistance.

    Domestic abuse
    it's the financial
    hook that gets
    every one of them.
    They'd be out
    ten times sooner
    if they could support
    themselves and their children.
      We deal with that
      three times a day.

They don't care
what you're going through.
    The plate glass window.
    I don't want
    to scream my name out
    in a room full of people
    I don't know.
      I don't want
      to say my name.
      I don't want
      to say anything.
      I don't want
      to be here.

A lot of women know
yes, he'll hit me
but I can
deal with him.
I can predict,
I can handle it
rather than
that scary world
being humiliated.
    To beg for money,
    to justify.

They do everything
to stop you.
Even though you
have a job
you don't have
the means to
insure your car,
put gas in your car.
You've got to
climb that mountain.

When I envisioned
this, my life,
it wasn't begging,
showing everything,
or do I have
any jewelry to pawn
before I can
get help?
    You just want
    to hide.
    This isn't right.
    This isn't normal.

Something like
transportation.
You've got to go
get the tickets.
You've got to go
back every week.
*You've got to
go get them.*

When you
bring a cheque
into the bank
and the teller
looks at you?
    You can see
    it right
    in her face,
    in her eyes.
You're always feeling
you have to
kiss people's asses
be grateful for everything.

It's like being
hit by a car.
All of a sudden
you're lying there
wounded from
head to toe
in every aspect
of the word
and now you've got
to fight for your life.

You have to
be able to
jump loops hoops
pound doors.
You don't have it.
You're surviving
from surviving.
It sucks.
You have to, though.

You've got to do
the running, paperwork
fighting. You cry,
you're angry.

You need information
resources, referrals
you don't absorb
take stuff in
so it has to
be reinforced.

It's so overwhelming
discontinuous support
systems, waiting lists
begging on your knees
crying at the bank.

If you yourself
working in the field
are frustrated
imagine a woman so
wounded?

And you're supposed
to go to work?
Raise your kids?
Go home and
make supper?
I don't know.

(names)

You want to
insult me?
Call me by
my married name.

It's been five years.
The school won't
recognize it.
Just getting your name back.
Your name!
It was the biggest thing
in the world.

I couldn't change
my kids' name.
I needed permission.

Finally he's
no longer knocking
at my door.

I'll never give
my name away again.

No way am I going
to go find him.

TRUST

In order to heal
you need
to trust somebody.
You need to trust
yourself.

Maybe I was
just fortunate I didn't
have that desire
to go back. Thank God.
I did go back
the first time.
I keep forgetting about that.
I keep forgetting about that.
All that brainwashing.
He had it
drilled in my head
that financially I couldn't.
How do you trust yourself?

Most say
I don't trust anybody
I have walls around me
but trust is
a relative thing.
One trustworthy person
helps the healing.

Rebuilding trust
is gradual.
Things in your upbringing
make it more or less likely,
faster or slower.

Trust the process,
trusting the client
to preserve their life.

Relationships?
They're out.
I cannot trust myself.

Our head is
incredibly brilliant
at deceiving us
all the time.

I scramble
to be worthy
of the trust
that's already given.

We don't listen
to ourselves.
Your gut
will lead you.

It's not about
me being trustworthy.
I am. I know that.
You don't.
You're not going
to feel that
all the time.

ARIA: STELLA

I look my
father's
spitting
image.

I used to think
who are these people?
I want to run
away from this.
    Everything so nice
    in deep denial.
    I didn't understand
    it was pretend.
Lovely people
very sick.
My whole life observing
getting red flags,
breaking up fights.
    Like being strapped
    to a bomb.

Mum attempted
suicide three times.

Sometimes it's terminal.

It took an immense
amount of tragedy
it was terrible what
happened in Yellowknife.

We were never together
again after that.

God had a hand in it.
If we had stayed,
I could have died.
I'm telling you,
that's what I see here.

My life was spared.

Mum drank
herself to death.

I found my
sister's body
in her apartment
eleven days later.

They don't hug you
they don't touch you
and there's her body
five feet from me.

They called the
victim crisis unit
she made me a cup of tea
and held me.

You don't know
how far that goes,
the kindness of strangers.

Viktor Frankl said
suffering ceases
to be suffering
in some small way
when it finds meaning.

I can backtrack.
I can see how
the chains, the links.

I am caught
between compassion
for him as a child
and hatred for
who he became.

There was abuse
in my home but
I choose not to yell
I choose not to
use a strap.

People do make
sense of their
experience, rightly
or wrongly.

Sometimes it causes
problems, sometimes it
leads to healing.

Some degree is possible
some of the time
but the big question
doesn't really make
too much sense.

I had a woman
say maybe I was
bad in another life
that's why it
happened to me.

Trying to figure out
why it happened
is accepting blame
on yourself again.

I don't think
it needs to
make sense.

The why isn't
every answerable
because the offender
doesn't say why.
Not very often.

Good people
can't fathom
the kind of violence
some people experience.

Almost always
there's childhood issues
sexual abuse issues.
Women say how
did I get
myself into this?
I say, you didn't,
you were set up.
Our society, the abuse
set you up.
We cannot in
any way blame
you for doing
what you've been
trained to do,
but it is
your responsibility
to look after
your future.

My bad relationships
stem back to childhood.
I can say it.
I know it's
not my fault.
I made these
choices because
of whatever circumstances.
My entire life
has gotten me here.

I don't think
I ever went
out of my way
to hurt another person.
What's the point?
Why would you?
At some point
I get so
tired of thinking.
That's his issue.
It doesn't say
a lot about
who I am.
Differentiate that.
I was socialized
into taking care
and he needed
me so I was
kind of hooked.

Something you don't
even remember
is extremely difficult
to understand.
I've got this
great brain here
likes to take a chunk
throw it out the window
and it comes back
every so often.

It's actually unbelievable
so not right
that it didn't happen
nothing in my
world prepared me
hard to speak
there aren't words.
Hearing the stories
is incredibly hard.
It upsets your world view
and can be a huge shock.
What is changes.
How can a person?
How is that possible?
We have some
theories, intellectually
we can rationalize it
but that's not
understanding it, really.

I don't need
to understand anymore
why I had a gun
to my head
did this drug
got into places
whatever.
That's what happened
but I don't
need to understand.

ARIA: BELINDA

The first thing I thought of
was my aura because
I want it to
bleed out all the time
because for me
it was constant.

It still is.
It's much better but
there's still a
helluva lot of
dark blue depression
green and black
the real shit.
All the shit
coming out of me.
The black is—I dunno.
Constipation.

I woke up
three days later
my mom said
you had a nervous
breakdown.
She goes, it's okay.
I took care of you.

This is years.
This is years.
This isn't
a day,
or something.
It stays really
mucky for
a long time.

One time coming
out from this
horrible, horrible
went to my mom's
my brain just
said, enough.

I was young
didn't have a clue
never questioned it.
It was normal.

This part is without
anyone in my life.
Not as much chaos
but it still
comes out everywhere.
Job, house, kids, whatever.
This is how it's going.
I'm still post,
if you ask me.
I'll be post probably
the rest of my life.
Post depression, post this,
post whatever.

I had to go
do these things
but my brain didn't
interfere with my feet.
It was probably
god-sent or spiritual.
My feet did it for me.
It took a long time just
to walk out the door.

My brain didn't work
I was so badly—whatever.
I did what was needed.
I didn't trust myself
for a very long time.

You get bursts
of happiness then
it just gets into
the shit again.

ARIA: CHERYL

This is a
very tumultuous
sixteen year journey
of finally being able
to see the light.
Having ground
around me, under me
most of the time
but sinking back
into the waters.

The only way
I was able to
let go was through
art, dance
body movement.
I had to let go.

Words weren't
working.

Art for me is
very simplistic
I actually hate it.
It is something
I have never
enjoyed.

I almost did
a numbers graph.

I started my journey
in the well
not realizing
I had been abused.

It took some time
to come to that
awareness.

Sprung out of it
broke free.

Then plummeted.
That first year
like I was drowning.
It was awful
after discovering awakeness
having to bury it again.

It wasn't as visible.
From my mom I got,
you have to treat
your man like a king.

Alright. Thanks
for that.

128

TIME

Women aren't cookie cutter.

There's a lack
of understanding
the time it takes
to even resume
a semblance of a life.

There's an expectation
if you're through
the court stuff,
you've got custody,
you're fine
but it may take 10 years
to recover to the point
where they can start
rebuilding their lives.

If somebody had mentioned
it might take another 15 years
it might have been easier.

I've done 15 years of therapy
and it's not ever
going to end.

It's part of you that died.

I truly believe
recovery starts in therapy
and ends in therapy
and you'll be in therapy
for the rest of
your bloodly life.
To me, therapy is God.

How the hell are
you supposed to afford it?

It's just about the money.
It's always about the money.

The people who are
making these decisions
need to come down
and follow a person
through what the system
actually does.

We've said that
for years and years
and years but
they never do.
It never happens.

Sometimes people are
in therapy for
a very long time
and aren't going anywhere
almost dependent on therapy
a kind of stuck-ness
like a bad marriage.

You only wish
you could keep
your counselor
in your pocket
keep her around
but she has
other work to do.
There are other people.

We beat ourselves up.
Why can't I work through this?
Why am I stuck?
Why am I crying?
All those stupid, negative
things.

I don't have time to cry.
I don't have time now.
I don't have time.
I don't have time.
I don't have time.

I'm tired. Always tired.
There. I'm done.
Time to move on
and all of a sudden
you fall back on your butt
again.

And you think,
    what's wrong with me?
    I must be depressed.

Knowledge is power
to make change.

Once you become aware
it's hard to become unaware.

If you live with that
for a time, let it effect
your decisions,
your future is changed.
Your feelings
eventually change too.

The important
beginning piece
is understanding
the kernel of abuse
is that they have no power.

Facing feelings,
internal responses,
what you allowed,
how you were trained,
what you can do.
Taking those steps.

I like to talk about
the effects of trauma
in plain language.
Hyper-reactivity
constriction
dissociation
depression
addictions
relationship problems
anger, denial, upheaval.
Ways of describing
that make sense.

A good medical evaluation
psychiatric evaluation
there is a lot
of co-morbidity
as we call it.
Could be depression,
substance abuse, psychosis.

I don't get
hung up on worlds.
My job is helping
the person name
their particular problems
encouraging reflection
within experience.

Labels are useful to me
in terms of treatment.

Diagnosis can be
insult or awakening.
Some say, I finally know
what's wrong with me.

It's not a doctor.
The doctor can't fix this.

What is trauma?
Something that shakes
you to the core
violates your self-esteem.
People don't come out
just normal from
something like that.

Most people with
mental health diagnosis
have historical child abuse
and adult trauma.

I come at it
from, well, probably
a feminist point of view.
    Me doing this work, yes
    but tomorrow I may
    need her help.
The two of you
working together
each with a
level of expertise.
    She was me
    but for the
    grace of God
    it could be
    us switching.
After all those years
working in shelters
the more I do
the less I know.

People need
to have hope
they'll get better.

I have faith.
I have seen successes.
You plant the seeds.
That's how it starts.
Hopefully. Hopefully.

I'm like a coach
a witness to hear
your story.
    I listen more
    than I talk.
    The woman
    guides the process.
    She lets me know
        what she needs.
A little kindness
and respect can
go a long way.
    Paying attention.
    I have this talent
    of writing and
    maintaining
    eye contact.
Noticing what
happened to you,
how you see it,
can we see it differently.
    Some teaching
    is involved.
If you were traumatized
as a child you may need
a childlike avenue to heal.
Our creative self,
there's a child for you.
    As long as it
    doesn't replicate
    the power dynamics of abuse.

How do you heal?

It will take time.
Every woman is different.
Everybody has to do
what they can with
the tools they are given
judging for themselves
what works for them.
That's all.

Start with the body,
the body is often
where trauma lives.
    Start with now.
    The present
    experience is your
    emotional state,
    whatever you are
    going through.
Once you're finished,
give it some time.
You get the
money back guarantee.
If you are not sure
you're quite there,
give me a call,
let's talk, let's meet.
    That would be ideal.

Physical, emotional
spiritual, relational.
    Different stages
    emergency
    out of whack
    suicidal, addicted
    all kinds of things.
To look at trauma
memories you need
a strong foundation,
a crisis plan. Trust
is absolutely essential.
    Some are not
    comfortable
    being pushed
    feel they're going
    to fragment,
    fall apart.

Aria: June

I like the beach ball
something I use to help
sexual abuse survivors
understand the process.

When you first
start to look
its overwhelming
a beach ball
right in your face.
The only way to see
anything else is
a supreme effort
to turn your head.

At some point
the ball sits
on the table
in front of you
all you have
to do to see
the rest of
the world is
turn your eyes
but it's still
at the centre of
what's going on.

Further along
the ball gets
put in a corner
of the room
most of the time
you focus on
other stuff but
now and then
it's still there.

You never really
get rid of it
but you can get
to the point where
you are in charge
of your life
and you choose.

The final stage
the ball goes
into the attic
it's still in your
consciousness but
you can choose
to look at it
or deal with it.

ABUSERS

There's nothing
they don't do.
They're like con artists.

When my ex walks
into the school
he's go this
whole façade going
I could just
spit on him
it makes me so mad.

It makes him look good
and me look
like a pain.

They don't know
who he is.

You think,
what made me
fall into that trap?

You're young
you're in love
you see the
little boy
inside them
but the shell
it's tough.

Always trying
to bring out
the little boy
as opposed to this
monster you see
all the time.

What kind of
relationship is that?
And you can't.

Forget the little boy.
Forget the little boy.
You've got to
see the man.

I come to a
point of realization
unfortunately he's lost
a little soul.

You can't change them.
I lost respect for him.
Once you lost that
you don't get it back.

It's pretty hard
to accept, you know.
You put me
through hell
and you sit there—
you don't voice but
things start changing.

He still tries.
It's *amazing*.
I shake my head.
What is it you
don't understand?

My greatest moment
was when I said,
you no longer control me.
This is my life.
He still doesn't understand.

The victim wants
the offender punished
to have treatment
the system to fix them.

I have very seldom
seen an abusive man
change his ways.

The shelter is
the first line of defense.
I've worked there
for 28 years.
    Every year we
    have more calls.

They've often said
    I feel I have
    a guardian angel
when they say that
when a woman feels
some level of spiritual protection
I feel so hopeful
really very positive
and it's just said
so many times, that.

I don't know how
people come to us
they go away
and they often come back.
    Nobody makes it
    on the first go around.

One of the things that dies
in a shelter is hope.
Hope for what
they've had in the past
and it's a terrible, terrible thing
to come to a place
where you have no hope
a terrible, desperate place.

Almost you have to
give up that hope
in order to make a new hope
but just that in between time
is extraordinarily difficult
and some women
don't get there.

I turned 65 this year.
I found I can't not work
I have such admiration
for the women.
I do.
Just to be able to go on.
Just, go on.

I don't know if
that's recovery but
one step in front of the other
is sometimes the
greatest act of courage
you can see.
Just, that.

134

ARIA: VICTORIA

The shelter workers
were a lifeline for me.
I was almost murdered.
I had a young daughter
and had a very hard time
with survivor guilt.
I was so badly hurt
I thought it would
have been easier for her
if I had just died
and he went to jail
and she had a chance at life.

You lose
part of yourself.
I lost a tangible thing:
partial functioning
of my brain.
I couldn't believe
he'd taken that too.
It was just
stunning to me
to lose part
of your functioning
just blew me away.

Two years later
I still thought
it was my fault
and I did have
counseling and so on.

For three years
I tried everything
to recover that part
then I got to acceptance.
Now I have to be
a different person
so what I am
going to do?

The shelter workers
really brought me back
they encouraged me to see
things can change.

All I wanted
all I have ever asked for
is quiet.
I just want peace.
I just want some peace.

We all want it better
for the next woman
so they don't have to lose
that part of themselves.
        It's a method of survival.

135

More affordable therapy.
People who are
well enough to be functional
are walking wounded.
Six sessions is really
not going to help
trauma very much.

First stage groups
second stage groups
then kind of nothing.

For a lot of women
the women's movement
groups and stuff
become the place
where they heal
find those supprots
build their trust.
        They get validation:
        you're not crazy,
        you're abused.
When you forget
why you struggle
that you're not alone
it's so easy to get
hard on yourself
to stay down,
be filled with anger.
    We need
    places of women
    where there is time,
    understanding, support
    to express, to rest, to be held.
It's so easy to forget
there's so many of us
while we have differences
there's comfort in
just being together.

We're not the problem.
        The problem is male violence.
        Buddy over there,
                somewhere he learned that.
It takes aman
challenging them, saying
no, you can't do that, dearie.
        Something meaningful.
        In their face.

All the stuff we have in schools
all themental health
all the ads
all the public ed
all the everything
it's not working.
It's not getting out to them.
Abusers don't listen to that.

        Education isn't enough.
        Programs for abusive men
        that focus on violence
        as a learned behavior
        have a one percent success rate.

        You have to touch the emotional part.

I think of
the school system.

Make violence
compassion, empathy
part of the curriculum
at ground level
as early as possible.

Kids know, not fair.
There's a sense
of anger with it
which I rather enjoy.
　　Never lose it.
　　It's precious.

We don't talk
about justice
in the curriculum.

Schools are so
apprehensive of
feminist agencies
because of the
stereotype.

Bringing guidance
counselors back.

Psychologists in
each and every school.

No waiting lists.
On the level
with the kids.

Not subject to
those damn budget cuts.

Just a right.
Male and female.
Paid full time.

I would like
to volunteer
to talk in schools.

Grade five, six, seven
someone coming in
reminding the next year.

I was never told
that you could say no.
It's okay. You have
your own life.
If someone tried
to make you
it's against the law.
Here's who you call.

It's not enough.
It's only out enough
to say we're
politically correct.

If I had learned
to put labels on
these terrible things
that abuse isn't normal.

The more often I got
raped, got hit,
got put down, whatever
I always thought
it was the norm.

The unfairness.
The unfairness.
Something is very
wrong in our world.
There's no justice.
   It's hard to
   believe what
goes on out there.
Why are we doing
so much post recovery
when the pre
is still not fixed?
   It amazes me
   the amount of times
   it still happens.
We think we're being
so progressive.
Women are still
not feeling good
   about themselves.
What is the norm?
The norm is often
what is abusing women.
   The names are put on
   to keep systems safe.
We are caught
in our time and
place in history.

I find the injustice difficult.
I bring it home.
Sometimes the anger
colors your world.
   I am tired
   of doing this work.
   I want it to stop.

You won't be angry
that other people
didn't do anything.
   You won't be angry
   at a system that
   doesn't work for you.
You won't be angry
at them. Get well,
shut up, go away.

   Sometimes the only
   means of protest
   has been through
   hurting yourself.

We are still collectively
beginning to tell the stories
of ourselves as women.
No more silence.
   Sheer grit and determination.
   As a group, no more.
   Never again.

This is your journey
but not just your journey.
It's the journey
of many women.
   I am the first woman
   born a person in my family
   while I'm old, I'm not that old.
The collective journey is important
if we want things to be
different for the next generation.

How do we change that?
One person at a time.

   A lot of times
   as women we look
   beyond ourselves
   and see there are
   people who have
   suffered more.

Recovery programs have
to be done in context.
We arent' just doing
it for ourselves.
This isn't a women's issue
it's the planet's issue.
What we see on TV
with other people
in books, movies. It's how
people view women.

The media is so
complicit in the status quo.

Anytime there's an
equality issue that
unites women in Canada
within the week there'll
be some documentary on
how bad it is in
some third world country
   almost to say
what do you really
have to complain about?
It could be worse.

We have this illusion
we've made it as women.

Scene Two: Assemblage

The choir of participants bows and sits. Sophie turns to face the committee, and speaks.

In a modernist project, this is where I'd lay out my findings and arguments, illustrated by anecdotes from these women, now read as primary sources, pinned and displayed under glass. I would elucidate my clear contributions to the glorious project of knowledge. As a postmodernist, I can scoff at such certainties while still craving them. Let us pretend, then, that knowing is possible, and truthful stories are tellable. If I could understand and explain what this means and why it matters, what would I say?

I would say that my findings speak to many issues, but, for the sake of this game, let's narrow it down to three. I might even give us headings to hold on to, like this:

Naming

The way women who have experienced spousal abuse are sorted and labeled has been well critiqued, particularly by Karen Kendrick.[274] Kimberle Crenshaw Williams points out that subordinated people also participate in and sometimes subvert the naming processes imposed upon them.[275] My findings suggest that women's ability to do so is constrained by several factors.

Women who have been in abusive relationships must present themselves as appropriately innocent and pathetic victims in order to access services. As Ubah notes, you have to appear meek and broken down in order to be believed and helped; you have to "look like an abused woman." This means you must not have "regained your power" (Ubah). Such women are expected to "kiss people's asses, be grateful for everything" (Tammy). The social institutions serving survivors rely on simple categorizations which erase the complexity and, often, the agency of the "victims." Olive observes, "the names are put on to keep systems safe." Many women thus express ambivalence about being seen as survivors or recovering.

However, the process of being named may be internalized as well as resisted. For instance, Jen says, "I must be naïve. I never looked at it as recovering. I understand now. I do." She finds fault with herself, rather than the adequacy of the label. This deference is sustained by our need for validation; like Tammy, we "need to know. Was it? Am I?" Our impossible histories leave us feeling like we are "going crazy" (Tammy). If the social institutions we depend on for material support and the therapists we turn to for emotional support both explain and frame our experience in terms of abuse, survival and recovery, those labels become powerful and hard to question. Many participants expressed discomfort with the prevailing terms but found it difficult to even imagine alternative labels.

This could be a bit like putting on a pair of shoes that pinch and chafe but "go" with your outfit. We may, on some level, like these labels. After all, being a survivor sounds tough and hardy, as if our lives were some sort of extreme sport. It makes everything we do seem "active and assertive when that is not always the case."[276] The language of recovery imposes a certain logic on what may otherwise feel like random suffering. Recovering is an optimistic verb; it suggests we are doing something, going somewhere, on a journey that can be predicted and which will eventually end. The labels don't quite fit but at least we have something to wear.

The problem is that, like ill-fitting shoes, the labels can make you bleed. Performing the role of a recovering abuse survivor in response to these external and internal pressures can provoke a sense of fraudulence, alienation and resentment that compounds our difficulties with trust. Walking too far in these labels can hurt and deform. Those who would seek to help us must, therefore, be much more tentative and careful in naming, recognizing that the prevailing terms are not neutral and do not arise naturally from our experience. The gap between signifier and signified may be inevitable, but it must not be ignored.

Testimony

The second issue my findings speak to is the problems of testimony and memory. Several participants described their memories as unreliable. As Belinda puts it, "I've got a great brain here, that just likes to take a chunk and throw it out the window. And it comes back every so often." Dawn says, "Our head is incredibly brilliant at deceiving us all the time." Jen, who asserts that she is not haunted— "I don't think everyone loses themselves"—also describes, with wonder, how she continually forgets that she is no longer in the marital home, reaching for the coffee in the wrong cupboard, or seeking the vacuum cleaner she left behind three years ago. She says, "Maybe I was just fortunate I didn't have that desire to go back. Thank God." When her therapist reminds her that she did, in fact, go back the first time, she shakes her head. "I keep forgetting about that," Jen says. "I keep forgetting about that. All that brainwashing. He had it drilled in my head that financially, I couldn't."

The participants thus seem to be both affirming and demonstrating the problems with trauma testimony and memory which are well debated in the secondary literature, and which I have discussed earlier. However, none of them seem to experience remembering and telling their stories, in the context of our group interviews, as problematic. In this text, I have similarly offered an apparently smooth and trustworthy narrative, even as I describe the impossibility of such accounts. All of us seem able to know and tell what happened to us. Even Jen, notwithstanding her slip, remains confident in the truth and validity of her own testimony.

The question of the reliability and possibility of testimony thus sits in tension. It seems disrespectful, if not politically and ethically irresponsible, to decide that a narrator who believes herself to be reliable is actually not, particularly when we sit in a position of relative power, and her narrative has been given to us as a gift. At the same time, it seems intellectually dishonest to presume that our testimony—even my own—is unproblematically accurate. As Peter Hodgins notes, our memory is inescapably "shaped by the present context and imperatives."[277] Testimony may work through a sort of placebo effect, rendered potent by our belief in it, rather than its substance, but I balk at the willful delusion this invites. The way out of this impasse may be to see ourselves as somehow simultaneously reliable and unreliable, or to find less dichotomous terms in which to think about truth.

Recovery

I could, perhaps most importantly, offer findings concerning the ethical and practical shortcomings of the recovery paradigm. As this is a complex issue, I'd need to unpack it in pieces.

The first piece relates to the problem of making sense. The recovery paradigm rests on the assumption that understanding our losses is both possible and necessary. The service providers I spoke with who aim to "help" us with this task position themselves as peers, doctors, coaches, witnesses or teachers. They are generally confident that knowledge or comprehension constitutes "the power to make change" (June) and that changing our thinking will, eventually, lead to changing our feelings. They see themselves as receiving and demystifying our memories in order to render our experiences understandable.

All of the participants in this study—we're just playing, so let's not call us *subjects*—have had a lot of therapy. This could be read as indicating our faith in the recovery paradigm. However, many of us still doubt that abuse could ever make sense. As Olive notes, "We have some theories, intellectually, but that's not understanding it, really." After fourteen years of therapy, Belinda says, "I don't need to understand anymore." This may be read as acceptance, but seems more like a sort of epistemic despair. She adds, "I will never recover." For many of us, making sense is not working.

Part the problem may lie in how we have positioned our abusers. Alice points out that our experiences are inexplicable because "the offender doesn't say why." Abusers, predictably, do not affirm, and often actively undermine, any explanation in which they are implicated. We collude in letting abusers off the hook by adopting explanatory models that hinge on the internal and social conditions which set us up. Our childhood sexual abuse, socialization as compassionate caregivers, or the ways in which we have done what we were trained to do (June) may be important pieces of the puzzle, but we allow them to displace the abuser who will not, or perhaps can not, explain himself.

This both obscures the centrality of the agency of the abuser, and shifts responsibility onto the survivor. Belinda says, "I can say it. I know it's not my fault," but there is a gap between knowing and feeling. If, "because of whatever circumstances, my entire life has gotten me here" (Belinda), then our lives, our choices, are at least part of the problem. Explaining as a process of finding out what is wrong with you may help you see what you can change, but it can also involve "accepting blame onto yourself again" (Belinda).

The tendency to blame survivors is perpetuated by the recovery paradigm's reliance on formulas that reduce the post-abuse journey to a series of predictable and manageable steps. My participants describe and draw their post-abuse processes as "not really linear" (Dawn), a circular journey or maze full of dead-ends (Margo), or a zig-zag path that loops back on itself (Cheryl, Alexa). Their process is not tidy and sequential; as Jen explains, you may appear to be "traveling from spot to spot" while "in your head you're all over the place."

Nonetheless, the dominant recovery models outline a series of interlocking, cumulative steps, leading upwards to various articulations of recovery, achieved by the survivor through adjustments in her attitudes and perceptions in a process reminiscent of feminist consciousness raising.[278] As Molly Andrews argues, many scholars, feminist and otherwise, "believe that most people lack the critical and analytic tools to make sense of their lives."[279] She notes that Stanley and Wise's (1983) observation of a three-stage model, beginning with false consciousness and moving in a linear progression through raised and finally feminist consciousness, is still apt. Even feminist therapy, with its focus on equalizing power relations and ostensible refusal to blame the victims, relies on a process in which the steps of recovery can be clearly and externally explained, and the survivor heals through changing herself. This tendency to simultaneously privilege survivors as the experts on our own lives and chart out for us the paths to our healing and enlightenment reflects a pervasive cognitive dissonance which must be surfaced and negotiated if we are to arrive at effective strategies for "helping." However, this sort of reckoning may be unlikely, as "even those who critique this hierarchical model of consciousness cannot resist placing themselves within it, at the highest level."[280]

Karen Kendrick confirms that a sort of false consciousness is often ascribed to survivors, which both homogenizes our experience and confers expert power (true consciousness) on an external other.[281] Recovery thus becomes a process of enlightenment that mothers are morally obligated to undergo in order to protect their children from cycles of violence. By extension, our non-recovery also becomes our fault. We are supposed to make "an internal commitment" to make time to look at it, to do the work (Alexa). You can "carry on or you can let it make you stop" (Shirley). You have to "want to let that go." If "I heal because I want to heal, I want to move on" (Jen), my *not* healing can only be seen as the result of a failure of will, courage, grit, self-control, or strength. My need for decades, or even a lifetime, of expensive counseling is attributed to my weaknesses or injuries, rather than shortcomings in the therapeutic constructs and tools with which I am being served.

Peter Hodgins argues that one of the major reasons we go back to the past (imagined or otherwise), unearth the dead and force them to speak again is that we want answers to the questions of "how did we get into this mess?" and, perhaps more important, "who is to blame?" This blame-seeking around events construed as pivotal "allows the chaos of the past *and* the present to be reordered into stable binaries of authentic/simulated, heroes/villains and victims/oppressors."[282] Our desire for such stable dichotomous stories often trumps our need for absolution, as we would rather be guilty agents than vulnerable and uncertain. This inclines us to accept theories which attribute our experiences to characterological and behavioral flaws which may not be our "fault" but are nonetheless ours to fix. As June explains,

"We cannot in any way blame you for doing what you've been trained to do. But it is your responsibility to look after your future."

Patti Lather points out that "theory is too often used to protect us from the awesome complexity of the world."[283] The project of "making sense" presumes a hierarchy of consciousness, in which the intellect can encompass and demystify profoundly emotional, somatic, relational experiences. It reveals the extent of our attachment to rational, dichotomous, orderly explanations. Like Cinderella's stepsisters, we would cut off our own unruly toes and heels in order to fit within these crippling paradigms—the modernist scaffold in which we are hanging. No wonder, then, that Olive says "recovery has almost a cruel sound to it."

[I could give you a subheading here, but I'm really not allowed to discuss it with you; I'm invisible and certain, clear and masterful, so sensible you could read me with your eyes closed.]

The second, related piece of what's wrong with the recovery paradigm has to do with its reinforcement of the status quo. Jenny Edkins observes that the survivor seeks resistance, but is confronted by state-supported normalization and medicalization:

> The aim is recovery, or the reinsertion of survivors into structures of power. Survivors are helped to verbalise and narrate what has happened to them; they receive counseling to help them accommodate once more to the social order and reform relationships of trust.... If this fails, then the status of victim of post traumatic stress disorder serves to render the survivor more or less harmless to existing power structures. In contemporary culture victimhood offers sympathy and pity in return for the surrender of any political voice.[284]

Ubah observes that this political silencing is enforced; "You must follow the norms a certain way you're supposed to, or else." Well-behaved survivors should tell their stories, truthfully, but only when appropriate; undue interest in our past trauma may be seen as an indulgent dementia, possession by ghosts, or a calculated (and suspect) effort to mobilize support for particular interests.[285] If we have children, we should develop business-like co-parenting relationships with our abusers, sitting sweetly beside them in parent-teacher interviews. Like Tammy, we cannot spit when they lie. We should work to put our experiences away, like June's image of a beach ball in the attic, and we should not be angry. Olive explains, "You won't be angry that other people didn't do anything. You won't be angry at a system that doesn't work for you. You won't be angry at *them*.... Get well, shut up, go away."

Karen Kendrick notes that one of the most damaging aspects of the recovery paradigm is that it foregrounds women's emotional needs over their material ones, as if, through personal transformation, we could feed our children and move on with our lives.[286] In practice, we often defer our emotional needs to address more pressing and intractable resource problems, such as poverty, unemployment, inadequate housing, and substance abuse.[287] In this inquiry, the need identified as most pressing is *not* personal healing; it is financial security. Because we have been at home with our babies, or financial control was part of our abuse, or we've had to leave our jobs (because we've moved, or he's stalking us, or our children have gone wild with grief), or perhaps just because we are women in a sexist economy, many of us end up "crying at the bank" (Victoria). We are supposed to accept gratefully the disrespect that comes with being a beneficiary of social services, the dehumanizing and demanding systems by which Canadian society manages and instructs the poor and marginal. We are supposed to accept the impossible social assistance levels and the insurmountable paperwork that comes with them, each page dripping in social stigma. Neoliberal economic policies, with their austerity agenda and social program cuts, have compounded the financial difficulties we face in our efforts to move on. We move from one system of fear and control to another. Our failure as self-sufficient adults reinforces our sense of inadequacy and shame.

The challenges we face in feeding and housing our families often mean we don't have *time* to do the "work" of recovery (Tammy). We are supposed to recover quickly—within a couple of years—but many of us find this expectation unrealistic. As Victoria says, "It might take ten years to get to the point where you can start to rebuild your life. It might take fifteen years. It might never end." Our recovery timeline is shaped by financial considerations; the medical system seems unable or unwilling to provide long-term, stable mental health services, and ongoing private counseling is prohibitively expensive. If we fail to recover on time we are pathologized as depressed or dependent. "There's an expectation," Shirley explains, "if you're through the court stuff, you've got custody, you're fine." But many of us are not. As soon as we are "well enough to be functional" we become "walking wounded" (Dr. White). We are then perceived as failed survivors, like non-compliant patients.

Responding to the evidence of an unjust social order, as it manifests in women's lives, as a series of tragic or pathetic female emotional and mental problems is a longstanding cultural tradition, perhaps most notably exemplified by Freud's decision that the middle-class Viennese hysterics in his care suffered from their repressed desire for, rather than experience of, sexual abuse.[288] The emotional work of surviving is important and daunting, but it conveniently displaces the tangible needs and injustices in which the state is more directly implicated. "While we are being exhorted to focus on our feelings, a lot of people are falling through the cracks in our society."[289] The goal of the recovery project is our personal happiness. However, as Linda Kauffman argues, "My happiness, frankly, is not very important in the grand scheme of things. I never thought feminism was about happiness. I thought it was about justice."[290]

Many of us seem to agree with her. Despite widespread anxiety about the decline of feminism, and the personalizing, pathologizing tendencies of the recovery paradigm, all of the women I spoke with understand their experience as the outcome of an unjust social order, rather than a private mental health problem. Many place their experiences firmly in a social and political context, often in explicitly feminist terms. As Ubah explains, "The norm is often what is abusing women." We are left "surviving from surviving" (Tammy).

While we are not a representative sample, my participants' degree of political commitment is striking. For some, this is a coping method; we survive through our work to make "it better for the next woman, so they don't lose that part of themselves" (Victoria). As such, we call for broader, systemic solutions, such as anti-violence education and counseling in the schools, the establishment of women's centers, and a much greater focus on male violence. "We're not the problem," Alice explains. "The problem is male violence. Buddy over there, somewhere he learned that."

There is a fundamental disconnect between the politicized priorities of survivors and the often deliberately depoliticized policies and programs supported by state-funded social services. It is profoundly disrespectful to presume that what we need most is counseling when we are calling for concrete changes in programs and policies. We may be expected and pressured to appear to recover because our unhealed wounds reveal the cracks in the social order. Marlene Goldman thus calls for a refusal of mourning, due to its complicity in hegemonic strategies of assimilation, but pursuing a political survivor mission without attending to our own losses would seem irresponsible at best.[291] We should not have to choose between docile healing and masochistic activism. Some, like Judith Herman, try to reconcile the personal and the political within their taxonomies of recovery. Rather than seeking to resolve these imperatives, I see them as evidence of the layers of understanding which come into play when we navigate by the stars of trauma.

The recovery paradigm's lack of revolutionary or subversive impact could perhaps be excused if it actually worked. But—and here is my final point—I am beginning to believe that, by and large, it doesn't.

Survivors apparently need to have hope that we'll "get better" (Shirley). Most service providers thus express faith in our resilience, drive for life, and recovery prospects. However, they are not unanimous; some acknowledge that "the aftermath doesn't go away" (Margo). As June describes, "You can never really get rid of it, but you can get to the point where you are in charge of your life." Upon closer examination, their vision of "recovery" looks much more like coping with a chronic illness than "getting better." Recovery is generally defined in terms of managing the degree to which we are haunted by intrusive, controlling, and disruptive conscious and unconscious, narrative and somatic memories. We learn how to cope when, as Tammy describes, a door in your brain flies open and suddenly you're shaking. Like Bluebeard, we live with locked rooms.

A couple of important dissonances emerge. First, I am struck by the tension between the variable and modest terms in which service providers explain our recovery prospects and the absolute investment in recovery implied by their identities and careers. Their enacted commitments tend to obscure their stated reservations. For instance, Dr. White says, "I like the idea that people recover… but you don't necessarily…. You achieve wellness, maybe." At the same time, however, as a psychiatrist, her identity and occupation are premised on the idea that she can and will evaluate, diagnose and treat survivors of trauma. A similar tension can be seen in secondary sources such as Judith Herman's *Trauma and Recovery*. In this text, she admits that recovery may not be possible, and might never be complete.[292] However, by setting these comments within the context of a major work describing the process and stages of recovery, she undermines her own caveats. It is as if they are saying, "You can't do this, but here's how."

Likewise, some service providers' positions seem to drift. For instance, Shirley initially frames recovery as just like a broken bone which, after it is treated, is no longer painful and even stronger than before. She goes on to say, however, that you could always find the crack with an x-ray; things would be all right for awhile, but it wouldn't ever really be the same again. Then she muses that it might come back, like arthritis, so "you'd have to take care of yourself." I understand these mobile and layered positions as reflecting the inadequacy of the recovery paradigm, rather than shortcomings in the service providers.

The second and perhaps most interesting tension which emerges is that survivors seem to be three times more likely than service providers to be pessimistic about our recovery prospects. "You survive because you have to," Tammy explains. But the story is not coherent. Jen, for instance, sees herself as recovered and says she is not haunted, but also says that "memories can be dangerous. It's easy to fall into depressions." Belinda says, "I'm still post, if you ask me. I'll be post probably for the rest of my life. Post depression, post this, post whatever. You get bursts of happiness and then it just gets into the shit again." Nonetheless, like many of us, she visually represents recovery as a left-to-right, past-to-present process of gradual clearing, lifting, or brightening. These inconsistencies reveal the chafing of an ill-fitting metaphor.

Implications

The recovery paradigm thus seems to be failing, on a number of grounds. Many of its faults are common to modernist progress-narratives—including, I suppose, this scene. But if recovery is inadequate, how else can we understand the post-abuse process?

As Melissa Orlie explains, thinking can rely on reason if it must only account for "the world according to its reigning terms," but in order to transcend its boundaries thinking requires metaphors. "Metaphor bridges the gulf between the visible and invisible."[293] According to Hannah Arendt, metaphors turn "the mind back to the sensory world in order to illuminate nonsensory experiences for which there are no words in any language."[294] In metaphor, "something invisible within us deals with the invisibles of the world."[295] It is the primary way we can seek to speak beyond the edge of naming.

In this section, I have described the recovery paradigm as unethical in its imposition of labels, enforcement and proscription of testimonial practices, hollow promise of making sense, allocation of power and blame, reduction of complexity, and depoliticized perpetuation of the status quo. It is, perhaps, time to seek other metaphors. The best place to do so is within our own language.

I have been struck, in listening, by the number of times the women in this study, both directly and obliquely, refer to their experiences as a death. This is important because you don't recover from death.

You don't recover from death.

This may be why recovery, as a metaphor and as a project, doesn't quite fit what goes on in the years after leaving abuse. Our survival is a sort of autonomic response—"you survive because you have to" (Tammy). You resume a "semblance of a life" (Victoria). In the Western cultural repertoire, things which endure their own deaths and have a semblance of a life are zombies, vampires, angels, phoenixes, and ghosts. I argue that new possibilities would emerge if we reframed our post-abuse process in those terms, using the metaphors of the undead and spectral to imagine our way through stuck and narrow places.

The scholarly terrain of spectrality has been well trodden, with Derrida leaving perhaps the largest footprint. In her seminal work, Avery Gordon proposes haunting as a way of apprehending the density, complexity, constrictions and longings of our everyday lives, enabling us to honor and attend to "the things behind the things." [296] Gordon argues that "the ghost is not simply a dead or missing person, but a social figure, and investigating it can lead to that dense site where history and subjectivity make social life." [297] By nature, ghosts "are haunting reminders of lingering trouble." [298] She explains,

> What's distinctive about haunting is that it is an animated state in which a repressed or unresolved social violence is making itself known, sometimes very directly, sometimes more obliquely. I used the term *haunting* to describe those singular yet repetitive instances when home becomes unfamiliar, when your bearings on the world lose direction, when the over-and-done-with comes alive, when what's been in your blind spot comes into view. Haunting raises specters, and it alters the experience of being in time, the way we separate the past, the present, and the future. [299]

She thus ascribes to haunting many of the characteristics which others have used to describe trauma. However, she draws an interesting distinction between the two:

> Haunting is a frightening experience. It always registers the harm inflicted or the loss sustained by a social violence done

in the past or in the present. But haunting, unlike trauma, is distinctive for producing a something-to-be-done. Indeed, it seemed to me that haunting was precisely the domain of turmoil and trouble, that moment (of however long duration) when things are not in their assigned places, when the cracks and rigging are exposed, when the people who are meant to be invisible show up without any sign of leaving, when disturbed feelings cannot be put away, when something else, something different from before, seems like it must be done.[300]

Gordon thus imagines the confrontation with ghosts as at least potentially productive, offering "a profound and durable practice of thinking and being and acting toward eliminating the conditions that produce the nastiness in the first place."[301] As she explains, haunting "is a very particular way of knowing what has happened or is happening. Being haunted draws us affectively, sometimes against our will and always a bit magically, into the structure of feeling a reality we come to experience, not as cold knowledge, but as transformative recognition."[302] Haunting thus appears as a site of learning and change.

In this spectral space, rather than a "method of survival" (Victoria), perhaps we reach for a method of survivance. In Canada, this term is used by the Québécois to indicate the tenacity of francophone cultural persistence. Derrida borrows it to denote an afterlife that "no longer means death and the return of the specter, but the surviving of an excess of life which resists annihilation."[303] Native American literary theorist Gerald Vizenor deploys it as an active renunciation and repudiation of "dominance, detractions, obtrusions, the unbearable sentiments of tragedy, and the legacy of victimry."[304] Survivance and the spectral thus open up a way of speaking in between the reductive terms of glib recovery narratives and the pathos of irredeemable loss. They allow us to see June's "spirit which will not lie down" as a sort of quasi-volitional, sinewy endurance, something other than personal heroic pluck. To me, this offers an appealing and oddly hopeful way of perceiving the post-abuse journeys we undertake in the aftermath of death.

While many theorists indicate their doubts about the viability of recovery, they persist undeterred in explaining how we ought to pursue it. If, rather than recovering survivors, we are understood as women who have endured our own deaths, what we can and should do shifts in the direction of grief and accommodation. Patti Lather imagines this as a process of working the ruins,[305] resisting the impulse to immediately clean up and rebuild fractured structures of meaning in order to reinsert ourselves into them. In Anne Michael's description of the bombing of Warsaw, a survivor recounts,

> The very first shop to open up in the ruins of the city, during the very first days following the German occupation, perched on top of the rubble, in the snow!—was a florist's shop. Even before the abandoned half-wrecked tram that contained the first café, selling soup and ersatz coffee—there was the florist. All the foreign journalists marveled at it—such a sense of life, such fortitude, such spirit—all the drivel those journalists spluttered…. But no one said what was surely simple and obvious: you need flowers for a grave. You need flowers for a place of violent death. Flowers were the very first thing we needed. Before bread. And long before words.[306]

As Michaels explains, the flowers reveal "a desperate instinct to leave a mark of innocence on a violent wound, to mark the place where that last twitching nerve of innocence was stilled."[307] They find a way to speak of loss without obscuring it, drawing our attention to a death without the misrecognition implied in immediately trying to redeem or undo it. Rather than concealing the unspeakable, flowers "just made you look harder."[308]

Perhaps we are thus called to write flowers into the ruins. This means letting go of our familiar and inadequate conceptual tools—the bulldozers and shovels we use to order and contain our worlds. Recognizing loss as "the very force of learning"[309] changes what it means to make sense and be useful. In such spaces, ethical practice demands an aporetic suspension of "assured ontologies of the 'real,' of presence and absence, a postcritical logic of haunting and undecidables."[310] Rather than tidy linear narratives, we spin ghost stories that tremble with sorrow, rage and laughter, "encircling the trauma"[311] and taking up "failed accounts" as sites of opportunity and agency.[312] Instead of walking the treacherous path of recovery, we negotiate spectral journeys of survivance, "surprised by difference into the performance of practices of not-knowing."[313] As ghosts, angels, zombies, vampires, and phoenixes, we gain a range of vocabulary and metaphors for imagining and articulating ourselves into and out of our pasts and futures. We can stop feeling guilty for not feeling better. We can bear witness to our own deaths, and bring flowers, dropping their seeds into the dark clefts of our wounds.

Pauses, turning to ask the participants behind her.

Does that seem right?

The chairs are empty; the women have faded away during her speech, and are now entirely gone.

Act V
The Story Ends

Scene One: Pub

Sophie is waiting by the elevator, after her dissertation defense.

Ubersophie: *(to Metasophie)* Thank you for keeping your mouth shut.

Metasophie: I just want to go home.

David approaches. Sophie jumps imperceptibly.

David: Good job in there! Well done, Doctor Tamas.

David and Sophie hug. She looks away and shrugs.

Sophie: I don't know.

David: I've seen a lot of these things. That was very impressive.

Sophie: I just make it up.

David: We should celebrate. D'you have time for a drink?

Sophie goes very still for a moment, but smiles.

Metasophie: He smells good.

Ubersophie: Careful.

Sophie: *(to David)* Sure.

The elevator arrives; they get on together.

David: You know, Sophie. This is a world of wolves and sheep. And you're a wolf.

Sophie looks at David, saying nothing.

David: You're like me. Easily bored by stupidity.

Sophie: *(teasing)* I suffered through your class, didn't I?

David: You were completely intimidating.

Sophie: Me?

David: Absolutely.

David continues talking as they walk through the tunnels to the graduate student's pub. Sophie is not really listening; she is thinking.

Metasophie: He's just saying that because he likes your ass.

Ubersophie: None of your accomplishments mean anything.
        You just flirt with powerful men to get your way.

Sophie: I had to manage him.

Ubersophie: Using him.

Sophie: As if we're in charge, here.

Metasophie: I'm so scared.

Ubersophie: Cry me a river. You *love* this.

Sophie: Just go with it.

Metasophie: I don't want to make him bad.

Ubersophie: Then stop touching him. Brushing against his arm.
        What the hell is *that?*

Metasophie: What am I doing?

Sophie: What's *he* doing?

Ubersophie: As if you haven't seen this coming. Nice work.

Metasophie: He thinks I'm special.

Ubersophie: Oh, you are.

Sophie: Please, can I just have fun? Can it just be okay?

Ubersophie: It's *never* okay. You're acting out.

Metasophie: Oh, my God, why?

Sophie: We know damn well why.

Ubersophie: And yet you write this whole dissertation as if the
        problem is *them.*

Metasophie: That's not fair. You know it goes back to—

Ubersophie: I am SICK of your excuses.

Metasophie: You *know* how it is. Like there *is* no decision
        threshold. I'm not even *here*.

Ubersophie: You're pathetic.

Sophie: Just breathe. We're okay.

They have arrived at the pub. David turns to Sophie.

David:　Can I get you a drink?

Scene Two: Home

8:00 pm, Friday night.

*Dora, Ruth and Tahirih—three beautiful brown-haired girls, aged
10, 12, and 16—are cheerfully doing the supper dishes. The front
door opens and shuts.*

Sophie: I'm home.

The girls call back their hellos. Sophie enters the kitchen with a box.

Sophie: Sorry I'm late.

Ruth:　Where's Shawn?

Sophie: He had a meeting after work and then went to the gym.

Sophie dumps the box on the table.

Dora:　What's that?

Sophie: This *(pulling a wad of paper out of the box)* is my
        dissertation.

The girls gather around, cooing.

Tahirih: Wow! It's heavy!

Sophie: Not really, for a dissertation.

*Tahirih takes a copy and sits at the end of the table. She starts
reading.*

Dora: So are you DONE now?

Ruth: Does this mean you're going to be less grumpy?

Sophie: Never.

Ruth laughs and hugs Sophie.

Sophie: Did you have a good day?

Ruth: Yeah. Can I read it, too?

Sophie: Sure. *(taking out more copies)*

Dora: What page am I on?

Sophie: *(showing Dora in the table of contents)* Here and here. Just don't mark them up. I have to send them out for binding.

Dora takes a copy up to her bedroom. Ruth sits at the table with a copy, flipping through it to read the scenes that the kids are in and laughing at the cast list. Sophie crosses the kitchen, turns the kettle on, puts the last few dishes in the dishwasher and wipes the counters. She leans against the counter, waiting for the kettle, watching Ruth. Tahirih has gotten half way through Act One.

Tahirih: Oh, my god!

She looks up at Sophie, her eyes asking if it's true. Sophie nods and shrugs.

Tahirih: That's crazy. *(shakes her head and keeps reading)*

Ruth: What?

Sophie: It's about your dad. You might not want to read it. You might find it upsetting.

Ruth turns to the opening pages and starts reading the first act. The kettle boils; Sophie makes three cups of tea and brings them to the table. Ruth is very quiet. Sophie stands beside Ruth, one hand on her back.

Sophie: I wasn't sure if I should write it or not. I'm really sorry if it hurts you. Really, really sorry, baby.

Ruth starts to cry. Sophie slides into her chair, pulling Ruth onto her lap. Ruth keeps reading to the end of the act.

Sophie: I don't know if I did the right thing. I'm so sorry. What are you feeling?

Ruth turns into Sophie's arms and sobs, then straightens up.

Ruth: I'm mad.

Sophie: That's okay, baby. You can be mad at me.

Ruth: No. At Dad.

Sophie turns white. She strokes Ruth's hair.

Sophie: Now I feel like I should tell you every shitty thing I ever did, so I'll have been fair. But I don't know who that would help. It might just make it worse.

Ruth: I don't want you to. I know you're not perfect. But why did he *do* that?

Sophie: I don't know baby. What is making you angry?

Ruth: It's like we didn't matter.

Tahirih looks up at Sophie, shrugs, and keeps reading.

9:30 pm

Dora is half asleep in bed, with Cricket nuzzled under the covers, a fat white cat on her pillow, and a thin black cat by her feet. The dissertation is in a sloppy stack on her bedside table. Sophie sits on the edge of her bed and leans down for a hug and a kiss.

Sophie: G'night, muffin.

Dora: Night.

Sophie: Did you make any headway?

Dora: A little. *(smiles apologetically)* I got tired.

Sophie: That's okay.

Dora: Is that actually what happened with Dad?

Sophie: Yes.

Dora: Huh. *(pause)* That's really cool, how you used you and Dad.

Sophie: Really?

Dora: Oh, yah. You are *way* cooler than the other moms. *(rolling her eyes)* You should MEET them.

11:00 pm

Tahirih is still at the kitchen table, reading, a half cup of cold tea in front of her.

Sophie: Go to bed, hon. You can finish in the morning.

11:30 pm

Shawn and Sophie are sitting facing each other, legs intertwined, in a deep rectangular tub full of hot bubbly water. A few candles flicker on the stone ledge around the tub.

Sophie: I am so glad we put in this tub. D'you think we'll ever finish the reno?

Shawn: It's never finished.

Sophie: At least we got it livable.

Shawn: *(taking her foot in his hands and massaging it)* Are you okay?

Sophie: I don't know. I hate making Ruthy cry.

Shawn: She'll be alright.

Sophie: I already feel like a shitty mom.

Shawn: You always do.

Sophie: What if the ex's use the text to prove we're trashing them to the kids?

Shawn: What if? It's not like they'll take us to court over it.

Sophie: But we work so hard to make space for the kids to love them. It makes us look bad.

Shawn: Like I care.

160

Sophie: Should I have given it to Joe and made space for him to speak?

Shawn: Why?

Sophie: To make it seem fair.

Shawn: But it's not like you're really even presenting all sides of yourself, or the theorists, or anyone. You don't know his story. It's not yours to tell.

Sophie: And it wouldn't feel safe. Feeling empathy for him. I don't know—

Shawn kisses her instep, and continues the massage.

Shawn: Are you feeling guilty?

Sophie: *(dejected)* For leaving him.

Shawn: *(nods)* It's not really about him, anyhow. Or you. You're trying to tell a bigger story. Right?

Sophie drifts for a bit, caressing Shawn's thigh absent-mindedly.

Shawn: *(softly)* That feels nice.

Sophie: It's weird, going back through my records to reconstruct a life. You don't write down all the happy stuff. Like, during the reno. All the times we were drinking tea and singing along with the radio. Or how fabulous and witty the kids are. Like this. Or the times I jump you.

Shawn: I like THAT!

Sophie: Goofy. All the good times get erased. You're too busy having fun to write anything down and then it's like they never happened. All you're left with is the whining.

Shawn: I thought that was the art form you were pursuing. Whining for dollars.

Sophie pinches him. He jumps and laughs.

Sophie: Bugger. I don't even know how to write happiness without it seeming really banal.

Shawn: And then it doesn't seem real.

Sophie: It's real in the visual record. You take photos when you're happy, but you write when things are hard. Maybe it's a female culture thing. When I'm writing to a friend, it's always, oh, my god, I'm so stressed out, here's why. And then those are the stories you have. Life constructed as a set of problems.

Shawn: It's very flattering.

Sophie: I'm sorry, Shawnie.

Shawn: It's okay.

Sophie: I don't want anyone to think poorly of you. Or me.

Shawn: You write what you need to write. Nobody wants bad stories about themselves. And a ridiculous part of me *does* want glowy doe-eyes all the time. But I'm your partner. I know what we are. That's not what real relationships are all about. Real relationships are chaotic.

Sophie: Ours, anyways.

Shawn: Have you ever been in a calm or sane relationship?

Sophie: *(thinks for awhile)* Maybe. But they were boring, so they didn't last.

Shawn: Then we should last forever.

Sophie: I just wish I didn't focus on what's miserable.

Shawn: Right from the very beginning your work has been about trauma. That's not a happy topic. You're not going to find a smiley face in the middle of a pile of trauma. But you're always looking for the flippant remark, something funny to say to draw us out of the intensity of that moment.

Sophie: Why?

Shawn: I think the only hope you find is in writing. You want there to be hope in other things but the only thing that you trust might be your writing. You and the page.

Sophie: Hmmm. *(pause while Sophie thinks)*

Shawn: Did you need me to go get your laptop so you can write that down?

Ubersophie: Yes.

Metasophie: No.

Sophie laughs.

8:45 am, the next morning.

Sophie is working at her desk in her nightie. Tahirih appears in the doorway, bright eyed, in her pajamas.

Tahirh: I finished it.

Sophie spins her chair away from the desk to face Tahirih.

Sophie: What did you think?

Tahirih: Well, I skimmed the testimony lecture.

Sophie: That's okay. I say right in the text, it's kind of long and boring.

Tahirih: But it was really good. I really liked it.

Sophie gets up and hugs Tahirih.

Sophie: Thanks, T. That means a lot to me.

They go to the bathroom and brush their teeth together.

9:30 am

Sophie is back at her desk, typing. The girls are downstairs in the kitchen, making pancakes with Shawn.

Dear Participants

My complete dissertation is now up on the project website. You can feel free to download and read the text. It's not what I expected to write, so you may also find it a bit surprising.

Dissertations are usually only ever read by a handful of people. I am planning to produce other work based on what I've learned from you that will hopefully be much more widely useful or accessible. I would really like to hear any concerns or thoughts you may have about it.

I have a bunch of ideas about where to go next - I want to talk to more women, to get a better feel for how we see our recovery prospects. I'd like to develop some research-based theatre that could be used in communities to raise funds and awareness about abuse issues. I'm also thinking about a web-based project collecting images of the post-abuse process, and I'd still like to experiment with arts-based play groups for survivors. What I can do next will depend on my funding/jobs but I'll post updates from time to time.

I could not have done this without your support. I have learned so much from you, and I am eternally grateful for the generosity, time, and trust you have—

Dora appears at Sophie's elbow, startling her.

Sophie: Hey there.

Dora puts a cup of tea in front of Sophie and gives her a kiss.

Dora: Breakfast is ready.

Sophie: Thanks, bunny. I'll be right there.

Dora exits. Sophie turns back to her computer.

—shown, both to me and to this project. I hope you feel that I have respected *(pauses, deletes "respected")* honored your stories in the way that I have used them, and that you feel heard.

Shawn: *(calling from downstairs)* Breakfast!

Sophie: *(calling)* Coming! I'm almost done!

Sophie stands to go. The phone rings. She turns and answers.

Sophie: Hello?

It is a woman, around Sophie's age.

Curtain.

NOTES

1. Margaret H. Kearney, "Enduring Love: A Grounded Formal Theory of Women's Experience of Domestic Violence," *Research in Nursing and Health* 24 (2001), 271.

2. Henry Krystal, "Trauma and Aging: A Thirty Year Follow-Up," in *Trauma: Explorations in Memory,* ed. Cathy Caruth (Baltimore: John Hopkins University Press, 1995), 81.

3. Carolyn F. Swift, "Women and Violence: Breaking the Connection," *Work in Progress* 27 (1987), 3.

4. Judith Herman, *Trauma and Recovery* (New York: Basic Books, 1997), 116.

5. Cathy Caruth and Thomas Keenan, "The AIDS Crisis is Not Over: A Conversation With Gregg Bordowitz, Douglas Crimp and Laura Pinsky," in *Trauma: Explorations in Memory,* ed. Cathy Caruth (Baltimore: John Hopkins University Press, 1995), 256.

6. Bessel A. van der Kolk and Onno van der Hart, "The Intrusive Past: The Flexibility of Memory and the Engraving of Trauma," in *Trauma: Explorations in Memory,* ed. Cathy Caruth (Baltimore: John Hopkins University Press, 1995), 174.

7. Krystal, "Trauma and Aging," 81.

8. Leslie M. Tutty, "Identifying, Assessing, and Treating Male Perpetrators and Abused Women," in *Cruel But Not Unusual: Violence in Canadian Families,* ed. Ramona Allagia and Cathy Vine (Waterloo, ON: Wilfrid Laurier University Press, 2006), 375.

9. Herman, *Trauma and Recovery,* 94.

10. Krystal, "Trauma and Aging," 81.

11. Kai Erikson, "Notes on Trauma and Community," in *Trauma: Explorations in Memory,* ed. Cathy Caruth (Baltimore: John Hopkins University Press, 1995), 193–97.

12. Patty Kelly, "Trauma Narratives in Canadian Fiction: A Chronotopic Analysis of Anne Michael's *Fugitive Pieces*" (Paper presented at *Making Sense of Health, Illness and Disease,* Oxford, 2006), 5.

13. Herman, *Trauma and Recovery,* 87.

14. Herman, *Trauma and Recovery,* 87.

15. Janice Ristock, *No More Secrets: Violence in Lesbian Relationships* (London: Routledge, 2002), 80.

16. Alannah Earl Young and Denise Nadeau, "Decolonising the Body: Restoring Sacred Vitality," *Atlantis* 29, no. 2 (2005), 15.

17. Jody Ranck, "Beyond Reconciliation: Memory and Alterity in Post-Genocide Rwanda," in *Between Hope and Despair: Pedagogy and the Remembrance of Historical Trauma,* ed. Roger Simon et al. (Oxford: Rowman & Littlefield, 2000), 197.

18. Ristock, *No More Secrets,* 80.

19. Herman, *Trauma and Recovery,* 41.

20. Jenny Edkins, *Trauma and the Memory of Politics* (Cambridge, UK: Cambridge University Press, 2003), 4.

21. Herman, *Trauma and Recovery,* 87.

22. Jean Baker Miller and Irene Pierce Stiver, *The Healing Connection: How Women Form Relationships in Therapy and Life* (Boston, MA: Beacon Press, 1997), 78.

23. Karen Landenburger, "The Dynamics of Leaving and Recovering from an Abusive Relationship," *Journal of Obstetric, Gynaecologic, and Neonatal Nursing* 27, no. 6 (1998), 700–06.

24. Herman, *Trauma and Recovery,* 103.

25. J. Roy Gillis and Shaindl Diamond, "Same-Sex Partner Abuse: Challenges to the Existing Paradigms of Intimate Violence Theory," in *Cruel But Not Unusual: Violence in the Canadian Family,* ed. Ramona Allagia and Cathy Vine (Waterloo, ON: Wilfrid Laurier University Press, 2006), 130.

26. Miller and Stiver, *The Healing Connection,* 78.

27. Kearney, "Enduring Love," 271.

28. Gillis and Diamond, "Same-Sex Partner Abuse," 128.

29. Ristock, *No More Secrets,* 74.

30. Ristock, *No More Secrets,* 119.

31. Swift, "Women and Violence."

32. Ristock, *No More Secrets,* 114, 137, 115.

33. Ristock, *No More Secrets.*

34. van der Kolk and van der Hart, "The Intrusive Past."

35. van der Kolk and van der Hart, "The Intrusive Past," 172.

36. Susan Brison, *Aftermath: Violence and the Remaking of a Self* (Princeton, NJ: Princeton University Press, 2002).

37. Dori Laub, "Truth and Testimony: The Process and the Struggle," in *Trauma: Explorations in Memory,* ed. Cathy Caruth (Baltimore: John Hopkins University Press, 1995), 67.

38. Edward O'Neill, "Traumatic Postmodern Histories: Velvet Goldmine's Phantasmic Histories." *Camera Obscura* 19, no.3 (2004).

39. Cathy Caruth, "Introduction," in *Trauma: Explorations in Memory,* ed. Cathy Caruth (Baltimore: John Hopkins University Press, 1995), 5.

40. Sophie Levy, "'This Dark Echo Calls Him Home': Writing Father-Daughter Incest Narratives in Canadian Immigrant Fiction," *University of Toronto Quarterly* 71, no. 4 (2002), 874.

41. van der Kolk and van der Hart, "The Intrusive Past."

42. Nancy Naples, *Feminism and Method: Ethnography, Discourse Analysis, and Activist Research* (New York: Routledge, 2003).

43. Ruth M. Mann, *Who Owns Domestic Abuse? The Local Politics of a Social Problem* (Toronto, ON: University of Toronto Press, 2000), 195.

44. Mann, *Who Owns Domestic Abuse?,* 10–11.

45. Gillis and Diamond, "Same-Sex Partner Abuse," 113.

46. Diane J. Forsdick Martz and Deborah Bryson Sarauer, "Domestic Violence and the Experiences of Rural Women in East Central Saskatchewan," in *Violence Against Women: New Canadian Perspectives,* ed. Katherine M.J. McKenna and June Larkin (Toronto: ON: Innana Publications, 2002).

47. Marlene Goldman and Joanne Saul, "Talking With Ghosts: Haunting in Canadian Cultural Production," *University of Toronto Quarterly* 75, no. 2 (2006), 645.

48. Goldman and Saul, "Talking With Ghosts," 654.

49. Goldman and Saul, "Talking With Ghosts," 649.

50. Jodey Castricano, "Learning to Talk With Ghosts: Canadian Gothic and the Poetics of Haunting in Eden Robinson's Monkey Beach," *University of Toronto Quarterly* 75, no. 2 (2006), 801–13.

51. Herb Wylie, "It Takes More Than Mortality to Make Somebody Dead: Spectres of History in Margaret Sweatman's *When Alice Lay Down With Peter,*" *University of Toronto Quarterly* 75, no. 2 (2006), 746.

52. Jody Mason, "Searching for the Doorway: Dionne Brandt's *Thirsty,*" *University of Toronto Quarterly* 75, no. 2 (2006), 785.

53. Gerald Vizenor, "A Postmodern Introduction," *Narrative Chance* (Albuquerque: University of New Mexico Press, 1989), 13.

54. Castricano, "Learning to Talk with Ghosts."

55. Arthur W. Frank, "Between the Story and the Ride: Illness and Remoralization," in *Ethnographically Speaking: Autoethnography, Literature, and Aesthetics,* ed. Carolyn Ellis, and Arthur P Bochner (Walnut Creek, CA: AltaMira, 2002); Christine Bold, Ric Knowles, and Belinda Leach, "Feminist Memorializing and Cultural Countermemory: The Case of Marianne's Park," *Signs* 28, no. 1 (2002), 125–48.

56. Jacques Derrida, *Spectres of Marx: The State of the Debt, the Work of Mourning, and the New International,* trans. Peggy Kamuf (New York: Routledge, 1994), 11.

57. Susan Gubar, "Empathic Identification in Anne Michael's *Fugitive Pieces:* Masculinity and Poetry After Auschwitz," *Signs* 28, no. 1 (2002), 249–75.

58. Brison, *Aftermath,* x.

59. Brison, *Aftermath,* 111.

60. Brison, *Aftermath,* 116.

61. Jean Amery, "Torture," in *Art from the Ashes: A Holocaust Anthology,* ed. Lawrence Langer (New York: Oxford University Press, 1995), 131.

62. Joan Didion, *The Year of Magical Thinking* (New York: Knopf, 2005), 189.

63. Didion, *The Year of Magical Thinking,* 168.

64. Landenburger, "The Dynamics of Leaving and Recovering," 702.

65. Landenburger, "The Dynamics of Leaving and Recovering," 704.

66. Landenburger, "The Dynamics of Leaving and Recovering," 704–05.

67. Hannah Arendt, *The Origins of Totalitarianism,* (New York: Meridian Books, 1958), viii.

68. Arendt, *Origins of Totalitarianism,* viii.

69. Lisa Price, *Feminist Frameworks: Building Theory on Violence Against Women* (Black Point, NS: Fernwood Publishing, 2005), 79.

70. Price, *Feminist Frameworks,* 6.

71. Melissa Orlie, *Living Ethically, Acting Politically* (Ithaca, NY: Cornell University Press, 1997), 196.

72. Orlie, *Living Ethically, Acting Politically,* 197.

73. Marilyn Smith, "Recovery from Intimate Partner Violence: A Difficult Journey," *Issues in Mental Health Nursing* 24 (2003), 547.

74. Smith, "Recovery from Intimate Partner Violence," 568.

75. Landenburger, "The Dynamics of Leaving and Recovering," 700.

76. Herman, *Trauma and Recovery,* 158.

77. Herman, *Trauma and Recovery,* 211.

78. Herman, *Trauma and Recovery,* 178.

79. Herman, *Trauma and Recovery,* 207–08.

80. Laura Brown, *Subversive Dialogues: Theory in Feminist Therapy* (New York: Basic Books, 1994), 25.

81. Brown, *Subversive Dialogues,* 50.

82. Angela D. Henderson, "Preparing Feminist Facilitators: Assisting Abused Women in Transitional or Support-Group Settings," *Journal of Psychosocial Nursing & Mental Health Services* 36, no. 3 (1998), 25–26.

83. Mike Kesby, "Retheorizing Empowerment-Through-Participation as a Performance in Space: Beyond Tyranny to Transformation," *Signs: Journal of Women in Culture and Society* 30, no. 4 (2005), 2055.

84. Tutty, "Identifying, Assessing, and Treating," 386.

85. Dwight Conquergood, "Rethinking Ethnography: Towards a Critical Cultural Politics," in *Turning Points in Qualitative Research: Tying Knots in a Handkerchief,* ed. Norman K. Denzin and Yvonna S. Lincoln (Walnut Creek, CA: AltaMira, 2003), 365.

86. H.L. Goodall, *Writing Qualitative Inquiry: Self, Stories and Academic Life* (Walnut Creek, CA: Left Coast, 2008).

87. David Mamet, *Three Uses of the Knife: On the Nature and Purpose of Drama* (New York: Vintage, 1998), 43.

88. Mamet, *Three Uses of the Knife,* 39.

89. Elie Wiesel, "The Holocaust as Literary Inspiration," in *Dimensions of the Holocaust: Lectures at Northwestern University* (Evanston, IL: Northwestern University Press, 1977), 9.

90. Shoshana Felman, "Education and Crisis, Or the Vicissitudes of Teaching," in *Trauma: Explorations in Memory,* ed. Cathy Caruth (Baltimore: John Hopkins University Press, 1995), 16.

91. Felman, "Education and Crisis," 16.

92. Laub, "Truth and Testimony: The Process and the Struggle," 64; Claudia Eppert, "Relearning Questions: Responding to the Ethical Address of Past and Present Others," in *Between Hope and Despair: Pedagogy and the Remembrance of Historical Trauma,* ed. Roger Simon et al. (Oxford: Rowman & Littlefield, 2000), 219.

93. Levy, "'This Dark Echo Calls Him Home'," 876.

94. Laub, "Truth and Testimony," 64.

95. Herman, *Trauma and Recovery;* Susan Brison, *Aftermath.*

96. Dori Laub, "Truth and Testimony"; Miller and Stiver, The Healing Connection; Kenneth J. Gergen and Mary M. Gergen, "Ethnographic Representation as Relationship," in *Ethnographically Speaking: Autoethnography, Literature, and Aesthetics,* ed. Carolyn Ellis and Arthur P. Bochner (Walnut Creek, CA: AltaMira, 2002).

97. Krystal, "Trauma and Aging"; Orlie, *Living Ethically, Acting Politically.*

98. Carolyn Ellis, "Being Real: Moving Inward Toward Social Change," *Qualitative Studies in Education* 15, no. 4 (2002), 399–406; Douglas Flemons and Shelley Green, "Stories that Conform/Stories that Trans-form: A Conversation in Four Parts," in *Ethnographically Speaking: Autoethnography, Literature, and Aesthetics,* ed. Carolyn Ellis and Arthur P Bochner (Walnut Creek, CA: AltaMira, 2002); Levy, "'This Dark Echo Calls Him Home'"; Robyn Read, "Witnessing the Workshop Process of Judith Thompson's *Capture Me,*" in *The Masks of Judith Thompson,* ed. Ric Knowles (Toronto: Playwrights Canada Press, 2006).

99. Levy, "This Dark Echo Calls Him Home," 871.

100. Peter Reason and Hilary Bradbury, "Introduction: Inquiry and Participation in Search of a World Worthy of Human Aspiration," in *Handbook of Action Research,* ed. Peter Reason and Hilary Bradbury (Thousand Oaks, CA: Sage, 2006).

101. Laurel Richardson, *Fields of Play* (New Brunswick, NJ: Rutgers University Press, 1997); Frank, "Between the Story and the Ride"; Ellis, "Being Real."

102. Edkins, *Trauma and the Memory of Politics,* 5.

103. Jan Patocka, *Heretical Essays on the Philosophy of History,* trans. Erazim Kohak (Chicago: Open Court, 1996), 134–135.

104. Judith Butler, "Performative Acts and Gender Constitution: An Essay in Phenomenology and Feminist Theory," in *Performing Feminisms: Feminist Critical Theory and Theatre,* ed. Sue Ellen Case (Baltimore: John Hopkins University Press, 1990), 273.

105. bell hooks, *Talking Back: Thinking Feminist, Thinking Black* (Boston, MA: South End, 1989), 9.

106. Roger Simon et al., "Introduction: Between Hope and Despair: The Pedagogical Encounter of Historical Remembrance," in *Between Hope and Despair: Pedagogy and the Remembrance of Historical Trauma,* ed. Roger Simon et al. (Lanham, MD: Rowman & Littlefield, 2000).

107. Marlene Goldman, "A Dangerous Circuit: Loss and the Boundaries of Racialized Subjectivity in Joy Kogawa's *Obasan* and Kerri Sakamoto's *The Electrical Field,*" *Modern Fiction Studies* 48, no. 2 (2002), 362–88; Zuzana Pick, "Storytelling and Resistance: The Documentary Practice of Alanis Obomsawin," in *Gendering the Nation: Canadian Women's Cinema,* ed. Kay Armatage et al. (Toronto: University of Toronto Press, 1999); Ann Haugo, "Negotiating Hybridity: Native Women's Performance as Cultural Persistence," *Women and Performance* 7, no. 14–15 (1995), 125–41.

108. Eleanor Wachtel, "An Interview With Judith Thompson," in *The Masks of Judith Thompson,* ed. Ric Knowles (Toronto: Playwrights Canada Press, 2006), 45.

109. Edkins, *Trauma and the Memory of Politics,* 8.

110. Brison, *Aftermath,* 12.

111. Homi Bhabha, "Postcolonial Authority and Postmodern Guilt," in *Cultural Studies,* eds. Lawrence Grossberg, Cary Nelson, and Paula A. Treichler (New York: Routledge, 1992), 60.

112. Edkins, *Trauma and the Memory of Politics,* 15.

113. Jim Mienczakowski, "The Theatre of Ethnography: The Reconstruction of Ethnography into Theatre With Emancipatory Potential," in *Turning Points in Qualitative Research: Tying Knots in a Handkerchief,* ed. Norman K. Denzin and Yvonna S. Lincoln (Walnut Creek, CA: AltaMira, 2003); Susan Finley and J. Gary Knowles, "Researcher as Artist/Artist as Researcher," *Qualitative Inquiry* 1, no. 1 (1995), 110–42; Pariss Garamone, "Tellingsmiths: The Work of Planting Trees, the Politics of Memory," in *Wildfire: Art as Activism,* ed. Deborah Barndt (Toronto: Sumach Press, 2006); Anna Banks and Stephen Banks, *Fiction and Social Research: By Ice Or Fire* (Walnut Creek, CA: AltaMira, 1998); Richardson, *Fields of Play;* John Law, *After Method: Mess in Social Science Research* (New York: Routledge, 2004).

114. Kelly, "Trauma Narratives"; Naples, *Feminism and Method;* Levy, "This Dark Echo Calls Him Home."

115. Theodor Adorno, "Commitment," in *The Essential Frankfurt School Reader,* eds. Andrew Aratot and Eike Gebhardt (New York: Continuum, 1982), 312, 316.

116. Law, *After Method.*

117. Law, *After Method;* Graeme Sullivan, *Art Practice as Research: Inquiry in the Visual Arts* (Thousand Oaks, CA: Sage, 2005).

118. Maggie Maclure, "Telling Transitions: Boundary Work in Narratives of Becoming an Action Researcher," *British Educational Research Journal* 22, no. 3 (1996), 273–86; Sullivan, *Art Practice as Research.*

119. Herman, *Trauma and Recovery.*

120. Heather Lash, "You Are My Sunshine: Refugee Participation in Performance," in *Wildfire: Art as Activism,* ed. Deborah Barndt (Toronto: Sumach, 2006), 221.

121. Orlie, *Living Ethically, Acting Politically,* 2.

122. Ristock, *No More Secrets;* Eppert, "Relearning Questions."

123. Monique Tschofen, "Repetition, Compulsion and Representation in Atom Egoyan's Films," in *North of Everything: English-Canadian Cinema Since 1980,* ed. William Beard and Jerry White (Edmonton, AB: University of Alberta Press, 2002).

124. Brison, *Aftermath,* 11.

125. Roewan Crowe, "Crafting Tales of Trauma: Will This Winged Monster Fly?," in *Provoked By Art: Theorizing Arts-Informed Research*, ed. Ardra Cole et al. (Halifax, NS: Backalong Books, 2004).

126. Amy Novak, "Textual Hauntings: Narrating History, Memory, and Silence in *The English Patient*," *Studies in the Novel* 36, no. 2 (2004), n.p.

127. Peggy Phelan, "Reciting the Citation of Others; Or, a Second Introduction," in *Acting Out: Feminist Performances*, ed. Lynda Hart and Peggy Phelan (Ann Arbor: University of Michigan Press, 1993); Benjamin Shepard, "Play, Creativity and the New Community Organizing," *Journal of Progressive Human Services* 16, no. 2 (2005), 47–69; Novak, "Textual Hauntings"; Patti Lather, *Getting Lost: Feminist Efforts Toward a Double(d) Science* (Albany, NY: State University of New York, 2007).

128. Law, *After Method*.

129. Robert Louis Flood, "The Relationship of 'Systems Thinking' to Action Research," in *Handbook of Action Research*, ed. Peter Reason and Hilary Bradbury (Thousand Oaks, CA: Sage, 2006), 142.

130. Vivian M. Patraka, "Feminism and the Jewish Subject in the Plays of Sachs, Atlan, and Schenkar," in *Performing Feminisms: Feminist Critical Theory and Theatre*, ed. Sue Ellen Case (Baltimore: John Hopkins University Press, 1990), 169.

131. Thodor Adorno, *Minima Moralia: Reflections from Damaged Life*, trans. E.F.N. Jephcott (London: NLB, 1974), 89.

132. Liz de Freitas, "Reclaiming Rigour as Trust: The Playful Process of Writing Fiction," in *Provoked By Art: Theorizing Arts-Informed Research*, ed. Ardra Cole et al. (Halifax, NS: Backalong Books, 2004), 269.

133. Julie Salverson, "Anxiety and Contact in Attending to a Play about Land Mines, in *Between Hope and Despair: Pedagogy and the Remembrance of Historical Trauma*, eds. Roger Simon, Sharon Rosenburg, and Claudia Eppert (Oxford, UK: Rowman & Littlefield, 2000), 67–68.

134. Tzvetan Todorov, "A Dialogic Criticism?" *Raritan* 4 (1984), 72.

135. Homi Bhabha, *The Location of Culture* (London: Routledge, 1994), 323.

136. Patti Lather and Chris Smithies, *Troubling the Angels: Women Living With HIV/AIDS* (Boulder, CO: Westview Press, 1997), 154.

137. Judith Stacey, "Can There be a Feminist Ethnography?," *Women's Studies International* Forum 11, no. 1 (1998), 21–27.

138. Sherene Razack, "Storytelling for Social Change," *Gender and Education* 5, no. 1 (1993), 57.

139. Stephen Greenblatt, *Marvelous Possessions: The Wonder of the New World* (Chicago: University of Chicago Press, 1992), 14.

140. Eppert, "Relearning Questions," 228.

Notes

141. Goldman, "A Dangerous Circuit."

142. Herman, *Trauma and Recovery.*

143. Roger Simon, "The Paradoxical Practice of Zakhor," in *Between Hope and Despair: Pedagogy and the Remembrance of Historical Trauma,* ed. Roger Simon et al. (Oxford: Rowman & Littlefield, 2000).

144. Norman K. Denzin, "Presidential Address on *The Sociological Imagination* Revisited," *Sociological Quarterly* 31, no. 1 (1990), 13.

145. Brison, *Aftermath,* 57.

146. Ristock, *No More Secrets.*

147. Herman, *Trauma and Recovery;* van der Kolk and van der Hart, "The Intrusive Past."

148. Bold, Knowles, and Leach, "Feminist Memorializing."

149. Sigmund Freud, "Mourning and Melancholia," *Collected Papers, vol. 4,* trans. Joan Riviere, ed. Ernest Jones, (New York: Basic Books, 1917/1959).

150. Goldman, "A Dangerous Circuit," 368.

151. van der Kolk and van der Hart, "The Intrusive Past," 179.

152. Krystal, "Trauma and Aging," 85.

153. Rinaldo Walcott, "'It's My Nature': The Discourse and Experience of Black Canadian Music," in *Slippery Pastimes: Reading the Popular in Canadian Culture,* ed. Joan Nicks, and Jeannette Sloniowski (Waterloo, ON: Wilfrid Laurier University Press, 2002), 265.

154. Darlene Hantzis, "Reflections on 'A Dialogue with Friends': 'Performing' the 'Other/Self' OJA 1995," in *The Future of Performance Studies: Visions and Revisions,* ed. Sheron J Dailey (Annadale,VA: NCA, 1998).

155. Ristock, *No More Secrets,* 135.

156. Razack, "Storytelling for Social Change," 61.

157. Brown, *Subversive Dialogues.*

158. Razack, "Storytelling for Social Change," 61.

159. Caruth, "Introduction."

160. Herman, *Trauma and Recovery.*

161. Kristin M Langellier, "Personal Narrative, Performance, Performativity: Two or Three Things I Know for Sure," in *Turning Points in Qualitative Research: Tying Knots in a Handkerchief,* eds. Norman K. Denzin and Yvonna S. Lincoln (Walnut Creek, CA: AltaMira, 2003), 455.

162. Richard Schechner, *Between Theatre and Anthropology* (Philadelphia: University of Pennsylvania Press, 1985), 142; Linda S. Kaufman, "The Long Goodbye: Against Personal Testimony, Or an Infant Grifter Grows Up," in *American Feminist Thought At Century's End: A Reader,* ed. Linda S. Kaufman (Cambridge, MA: Blackwell, 1993).

163. Kaufman, "The Long Goodbye."

164. Naples, *Feminism and Method;* Pam Alldred and Val Gillies, "Eliciting Research Accounts: Re/Producing Modern Subjects?," in *Ethics in Qualitative Research,* ed. Melanie Mauthner et al. (London: Sage, 2002).

165. Orlie, *Living Ethically, Acting Politically,* 8.

166. Edkins, *Trauma and the Memory of Politics.*

167. Pamela Sugiman, "Memories of Internment: Narrating Japanese Women's Life Stories," *Canadian Journal of Sociology* 29, no. 3 (2004), 359–388.

168. Edkins, *Trauma and the Memory of Politics;* Ristock, *No More Secrets.*

169. Sugiman, "Memories of Internment," 364.

170. Erica Burman, "Fictioning Authority: Writing Experience in Feminist Teaching and Learning," *Psychodynamic Counselling* 7, no. 2 (2001), 9.

171. Marjorie L. DeVault, *Liberating Method: Feminism and Social Reseach* (Philadephia, PA: Temple University Press, 1999).

172. O'Neill, "Traumatic Postmodern Histories," 164.

173. O'Neill, "Traumatic Postmodern Histories."

174. O'Neill, "Traumatic Postmodern Histories," 164.

175. Kelly, "Trauma Narratives," 9.

176. Angela D. Henderson, "Preparing Feminist Facilitators: Assisting Abused Women in Transitional or Support-Group Settings," *Journal of Psychosocial Nursing & Mental Health Services* 36, no. 3 (1998): 25–33.

177. Brown, *Subversive Dialogues,* 133.

178. Turid Markussen, "Practicing Performativity: Transformative Moments in Research," *European Journal of Women's Studies* 12, no. 3 (2005), 329–44.

179. Lather, *Getting Lost,* 31.

180. Christine Halse and Anne Honey, "Unraveling Ethics: Illuminating the Moral Dilemmas of Research Ethics," *Signs: Journal of Women in Culture and Society* 30, no. 4 (2005), 2142.

181. Halse and Honey, "Unraveling Ethics," 2145.

182. Ristock, *No More Secrets.*

183. Alldred and Gillies, "Eliciting Research Accounts," 152.

184. Judith Butler, "Contingent Foundations: Feminism and the Question of 'Postmodernism,'" in *Feminists Theorize the Political,* ed. Judith Butler and Joan Scott (New York: Routledge, 1992), 9.

185. Richardson, *Fields of Play,* 62.

186. Butler, "Contingent Foundations," 10.

187. Sarah Pink, *Doing Visual Ethnography: Images, Media and Representation in Research* (Thousand Oaks, CA: Sage, 2001), 27.

188. Avery Gordon, *Ghostly Matters: Haunting and the Sociological Imagination,* 2nd ed. (Minneapolis, MN: University of Minnesota Press, 2008), 4–5.

189. Conquergood, "Rethinking Ethnography: Towards a Critical Cultural Politics."

190. Lather and Smithies, *Troubling the Angels,* 34.

191. Patricia Hill Collins, "Learning From the Outsider Within: The Sociological Significance of Black Feminist Thought," in *Beyond Methodology,* ed. Mary Margaret Fonow and Judith A Cook (Bloomington, IN: Indiana University Press, 1991).

192. Linda Tuhiwai Smith, *Decolonizing Methodologies* (London: Zed Books, 1999), 137.

193. Smith, *Decolonizing Methodologies;* Jolley Bruce Chistman, "Working in the Field as a Female Friend," *Anthropology and Education Quarterly* 19, no. 2 (1988), 70–85; Joan Acker, Kate Barry and Johanna Esseveld, "Objectivity and Truth: Problems in Doing Feminist Research," in *Feminism and Social Change: Theory and Practice,* ed. Heidi Gottfried (Urbana,IL: University of Chicago Press, 1999).

194. Liz Kelly et al., "Researching Women's Lives or Studying Women's Oppression? Reflections on What Constitutes Feminist Research," in *Researching Women's Lives from a Feminist Perspective,* ed. Mary Maynard and June Purvis (London: Taylor & Francis, 1994).

195. Chandra Talpade Mohanty, "Sisterhood, Coalition, and the Politics of Experience," in *Feminism Without Borders: Decolonizing Theory,* ed. Chandra T. Mohanty (Durham, NC: Duke University Press, 2003); Naples, *Feminism and Method.*

196. Donna Haraway, "Situated Knowledges: The Science Question in Feminism and the Privilege of Partial Perspective," in *Turning Points in Qualitiative Research: Tying Knots in a Handkerchief,* ed. Norman K. Denzin and Yvonna S. Lincoln (Walnut Creek, CA: AltaMira, 2003), 29.

197. Haraway, "Situated Knowledges," 22.

198. Law, *After Method;* Patricia Maguire, *Doing Participatory Research: A Feminist Approach* (Amherst, MA: The Centre for International Education, 1987), 37.

199. Mary E. Gilfus et al. "Research on Violence Against Women: Creating Survivor-Informed Collaborations," *Violence Against Women* 15 (1999), 1194–1212.

200. Henderson, "Preparing Feminist Facilitators," 29.

201. Brown, *Subversive Dialogues,* 22.

202. Liane V. Davis and Meera Srinivasan, "Listening to the Voices of Battered Women: What Helps Them Escape Violence," *Affilia: Journal of Women and Social Work* 10 (1995), 67.

203. Razack, "Storytelling for Social Change," 63.

204. Brown, *Subversive Dialogues,* 106.

205. Diane L. Wolf, "Situating Feminist Dilemmas in Fieldwork," in *Feminist Dilemmas in Fieldwork,* ed. Diane L. Wolf (Boulder, CO: Westview Press, 1996).

206. Orlie, *Living Ethically, Acting Politically,* 27.

207. Sandra Harding and Kathryn Norberg, "New Feminist Approaches to Social Science Methodologies: An Introduction," *Signs: Journal of Women in Culture and Society* 30, no. 4 (2005), 2012; Alldred and Gillies, "Eliciting Research Accounts," 152.

208. Lather, *Getting Lost,* 47.

209. Lenore Lyons and Janine Chipperfield, "(De)Constructing the Interview: A Critique of the Participatory Model," *Resources for Feminist Research* 28, no. 1/2 (2000), 33–48.

210. Wolf, "Situating Feminist Dilemmas in Fieldwork."

211. Jayati Lal, "Situating Locations: The Politics of Self, Identity, and 'Other' in Living and Writing the Text," in *Feminist Dilemmas in Fieldwork,* ed. Diane L. Wolf (Boulder, CO: Westview, 1996), 197.

212. Orlie, *Living Ethically, Acting Politically,* 4; Brown, *Subversive Dialogues,* 105.

213. Val Gilles and Pam Alldred, "The Ethics of Intention: Research as a Political Tool," in *Ethics in Qualitative Research,* ed. Melanie Mauthner et al. (London: Sage, 2002), 44.

214. Lois Presser, "Negotiating Power and Narrative in Research: Implications for Feminist Methodology," *Signs: Journal of Women in Culture and Society* 30, no. 4 (2005), 2007.

215. Richardson, *Fields of Play,* 32.

216. Gilles and Alldred, "The Ethics of Intention," 156.

217. Gottschalk, "Postmodern Sensibilities and Ethnographic Possibilities," in *Fiction and Social Research: By Ice or Fire,* eds. Anna Banks and Stephen P. Banks (Walnut Creek, CA: AltaMira, 1998), 222.

218. Deborah Britzman and Alice J. Pitt, "Speculation on Qualities of Difficult Knowledge in Teaching and Learning: An Experiment in Psychoanalytic Research," in *Doing Educational Research,* Eds. Kenneth Tobin and Joe L. Kincheloe (Boston, MA: Sense Publishers, 2006), 390.

219. Richardson, *Fields of Play,* 148.

220. Shepard, "Play, Creativity and the New Community Organizing," 50.

221. Lather, *Getting Lost,* 146.

222. Karen Potts and Leslie Brown, "Becoming an Anti-Oppressive Researcher," in *Research as Resistance: Critical Indigenous and Anti-Oppressive Approaches,* ed. Leslie Brown and Susan Strega (Toronto: Canadian Scholars' Press, 2003), 267.

223. John Heron and Peter Reason, "The Practice of Co-Operative Inquiry: Research 'With' Rather Than 'On' People," in *Handbook of Action Research,* ed. Peter Reason and Hilary Bradbury (Thousand Oaks, CA: Sage, 2006), 179.

224. Edkins, *Trauma and the Memory of Politics,* 5.

225. Pamela Cotterill, "Interviewing Women: Issues of Friendship, Vulnerability, and Power," *Women's Studies International Forum* 15, no. 5/6, 595.

226. Mary R. Harvey et al., "In the Aftermath of Sexual Abuse: Making and Remaking Meaning in Narratives of Trauma and Recovery," *Narrative Inquiry* 10, no. 2 (2001), 291–311; Maclure, *Telling Transitions.*

227. Jenny Horsman, "Literacy Learning for Survivors of Trauma: Acting 'Normal,'" in *Violence Against Women: New Canadian Perspectives,* ed. Katherine M.J. McKenna and June Larkin (Toronto, ON: Innana Publishing, 2002), 270.

228. Angela McRobbie, "The Politics of Feminist Research: Between Talk, Text and Action," *Feminist Review* 12 (1982), 55.

229. Kaja Silverman, *The Threshold of the Visible World* (New York: Routledge, 1996), 189.

230. Potts and Brown, "Becoming an Anti-Oppressive Researcher," 270.

231. McRobbie, "The Politics of Feminist Research," 55.

232. Cotterill, "Interviewing Women," 601.

233. Conquergood, "Rethinking Ethnography," 355.

234. Julie Salverson, "Anxiety and Contact," 72.

235. Marjorie L. DeVault and Glenda Gross, "Feminist Interviewing: Experience, Talk and Knowledge," in *Handbook of Feminist Research: Theory and Praxis,* ed. Sharlene Nagy Hesse-Biber (Thousand Oaks, CA: Sage, 2006), 182.

236. Erin Graham, "This Trauma is Not Vicarious," *Canadian Woman Studies* 25, no. 1–2 (2006), 19.

237. Herman, *Trauma and Recovery,* 69.

238. Felman, "Education and Crisis," 15.

239. Salverson, "Anxiety and Contact," 73.

240. Roger Simon et al., "Introduction: Between Hope and Despair," 7.

241. Salverson, "Anxiety and Contact," 73.

242. Salverson, "Anxiety and Contact," 62.

243. Lash, "You Are My Sunshine," 227.

244. Lash, "You Are My Sunshine," 227.

245. E.W. Eisner, "The Promise and Perils of Alternative Forms of Data Representation," *Educational Researcher* 26, no. 6 (1997), 8.

246. Mamet, *Three Uses of the Knife,* 50.

247. Mamet, *Three Uses of the Knife,* 25.

248. Douglas Foley, "Critical Ethnography: The Reflexive Turn," *Qualitative Studies in Education* 15, no. 5 (2002), 479.

249. Maura McIntyre, "Ethic and Aesthetics: The Goodness of Arts-Informed Research," in *Provoked By Art: Theorizing Arts-Informed Research,* ed. Ardra Cole et al. (Halifax, NS: Backalong Books, 2004), 256.

250. Yvonna S. Lincoln, "Engaging Sympathies: Relationships Between Action Research and Social Constructivism," in *Handbook of Action Research,* ed. Peter Reason and Hilary Bradbury (Thousand Oaks, CA: Sage, 2006), 127.

251. Nel Noddings, *Caring: A Feminine Approach to Ethics and Moral Education* (Berkeley, CA: University of California Press, 1984), 105.

252. Susan McDonald, "Asking Questions and Asking More: Reflections on Feminist Participatory Research," *Resources for Feminist Research* 30, no. 1-2 (2003), 77-100.

253. Gilfus et al., "Research on Violence Against Women," 119.

254. M. Brinton Lykes and Erzulie Coquillon, "Participatory and Action Research and Feminisms," in *Handbook of Feminist Research: Theory and Praxis,* ed. Sharlene Nagy Hesse-Biber (Thousand Oaks, CA: Sage, 2006), 301.

255. Sherry Gorelick, "Contradictions of Feminist Methodology," in *Feminism and Social Change: Bridging Theory and Practice,* ed. Heidi Gottfried (Urbana, IL: University of Chicago Press, 1996), 32; Lorraine Code, "How Do We Know? Questions of Method in Feminist Practice," in *Changing Methods: Feminists Transforming Practice,* ed. Sandra Burt and Lorraine Code (Peterborough, ON: Broadview Press, 1995), 23.

256. Gilles and Alldred, "The Ethics of Intention," 45.

257. Tim Prentki and Jan Selman, *Popular Theatre in Political Culture: Britain and Canada in Focus* (Bristol, UK: Intellect Books, 2000), 158.

258. Francesca M. Cancian, "Participatory Research and Alternative Strategies for Activist Sociology," in *Feminism and Social Change: Bridging Theory and Practice,* ed. Heidi Gottfried (Urbana, IL: University of Chicago Press, 1996), 192.

259. Margaret Randall, *When I Look Into the Mirror and See You: Women,*

Terror and Resistance (New Brunswick, NJ: Rutgers University Press, 2003), 195.

260. Molly Andrews, "Feminist Research With Non-Feminist and Anti-Feminist Women: Meeting the Challenge," *Feminism & Psychology* 12, no. 1 (2002), 60.

261. Salverson, "Anxiety and Contact," 68.

262. Salverson, "Anxiety and Contact," 67–68.

263. Dominic LaCapra, "Trauma, Absence, Loss," *Critical Inquiry* 25, no. 4 (Summer 1999), 699.

264. Cotterill, "Interviewing Women," 598.

265. Eppert, "Relearning Questions," 228.

266. John Rowan, "The Humanistic Approach to Action Research," in *Handbook of Action Research,* ed. Peter Reason and Hilary Bradbury (Thousand Oaks, CA: Sage, 2006), 116; Lash, "You Are My Sunshine," 225.

267. Orlie, *Living Ethically, Acting Politically,* 174.

268. McRobbie, "The Politics of Feminist Research," 52.

269. Mamet, *Three Uses of the Knife,* 18.

270. Beverley Skeggs, "Situating the Production of Feminist Ethnography," in *Researching Women's Lives from a Feminist Perspective,* ed. Mary Maynard and June Purvis (London: Taylor & Francis, 1994), 79.

271. Horsman, "Literacy Learning for Survivors of Trauma," 269.

272. Lash, "You Are My Sunshine," 221.

273. Law, *After Method.*

274. Karen Kendrick, "Producing the Battered Woman," in *Community Activism and Feminist Politics: Organizing Across Race, Class and Gender,* ed. Nancy Naples (New York: Routledge, 1998).

275. Kimberle Crenshaw Williams, "Mapping the Margins: Intersectionality, Identity Politics, and Violence Against Women of Color," *Stanford Law Review* 43, no. 6 (1991), 1297.

276. Ristock, *No More Secrets,* 94.

277. Peter Hodgins, "Our Haunted Present: Cultural Memory in Question," *Topia: Canadian Journal of Cultural Studies* 12 (2004), 101.

278. See, for instance, Tutty, "Identifying, Assessing, and Treating"; Landenburger, "The Dynamics of Leaving and Recovering"; Smith, "Recovery From Intimate Partner Violence"; or Judith Wuest and Marilyn Merritt-Gray, "Not Going Back: Sustaining the Separation in the Process of Leaving Abusive Relationships," *Violence Against Women* 5, no. 2 (1999), 110–33.

279. Andrews, "Feminist Research," 57.

280. Andrews, "Feminist Research," 58.

281. Kendrick, "Constructing the Battered Woman," 170.

282. Hodgins, "Our Haunted Present," 100.

283. Patti Lather, "Research as Praxis," *Harvard Educational Review* 56, no. 3 (1986), 267.

284. Edkins, *Trauma and the Memory of Politics*, 9.

285. Roger Simon et al., "Introduction: Between Hope and Despair," 2.

286. Kendrick, "Producing the Battered Woman," 159.

287. Tutty, "Identifying, Assessing, and Treating," 389.

288. For a full description of this turn, see Judith Herman, *Trauma and Recovery*, 18–19.

289. Kauffman, "The Long Goodbye," 270.

290. Kauffman, "The Long Goodbye," 274.

291. Goldman, "A Dangerous Circuit," 368.

292. Herman, *Trauma and Recovery*, 211.

293. Orlie, *Living Ethically, Acting Politically*, 163.

294. Hannah Arendt, *Life of the Mind, Vol.1* (New York: Harcourt Brace, 1978), 106.

295. Arendt, *Life of the Mind*, 123.

296. Gordon, *Ghostly Matters*, 8.

297. Gordon, *Ghostly Matters*, 8.

298. Gordon, *Ghostly Matters*, xix.

299. Gordon, *Ghostly Matters*, xvi.

300. Gordon, *Ghostly Matters*, xvi.

301. Gordon, *Ghostly Matters*, xvii.

302. Gordon, *Ghostly Matters*, 8.

303. Jacques Derrida, *Archive Fever: A Freudian Impression* (Chicago, IL: University of Chicago Press, 1996), 60.

304. Gerald Vizenor, "Aesthetics of Survivance: Literary Theory and Practice," in *Survivance: Narratives of Native Presence*, ed. Gerald Vizenor (Lincoln, NE: University of Nebraska Press, 2008), 1.

305. Lather, *Getting Lost*, 13.

306. Anne Michaels, *The Winter Vault* (Toronto: McClelland & Stewart, 2009), 217–218.

307. Anne Michaels, *The Winter Vault*, 217.

308. Judith Thompson, *The Crackwalker* (Toronto: Playwrights Canada Press,

1980), 74.

309. Lather, *Getting Lost,* 13.

310. Lather, *Getting Lost,* 6.

311. Edkins, *Trauma and the Memory of Politics,* 15.

312. Lather, *Getting Lost,* 39.

313. Lather, *Getting Lost,* 7.

CAST

Acker, Joan, Kate Barry, and Johanna Esseveld. "Objectivity and Truth: Problems in Doing Feminist Research." In *Feminism and Social Change: Bridging Theory and Practice,* edited by Heidi Gottfried, 60–87. Urbana, IL: University of Chicago Press, 1996.

Adorno, Theodor. *Minima Moralia: Reflections from a Damaged Life.* Translated by E. F. N. Jephcott. London: NLB, 1974.

———. "Commitment." In *The Essential Frankfurt School Reader,* edited by Andrew Aratot and Eike Gebhardt, 300–18. New York: Continuum, 1982.

Alexa. Is teaching herself how to paint.

Alice. Plays soccer.

Alldred, Pam, and Val Gillies. "Eliciting Research Accounts: Re/Producing Modern Subjects?" In *Ethics in Qualitative Research,* edited by Melanie Mauthner, Maxine Birch, Julie Jessop, and Tina Miller, 146–65. London: Sage, 2002.

Amery, Jean. "Torture." In *Art From the Ashes: A Holocaust Anthology,* edited by Lawrence Langer, 119–36. New York: Oxford University Press, 1995.

Andrews, Molly. "Feminist Research with Non-Feminist and Anti-Feminist Women: Meeting the Challenge." *Feminism & Psychology* 12, no. 1 (2002), 55–77.

Angel. I still wish we could talk.

Anna. Has grandchildren.

Anne. Raises horses.

Arendt, Hannah. *The Origins of Totalitarianism*. New York: Meridian Books, 1958.

———. *Life of the Mind*. Vol. 1, New York: Harcourt Brace, 1978.

Banks, Anna, and Stephen Banks. *Fiction and Social Research: By Ice or Fire*. Walnut Creek, CA: AltaMira, 1998.

Barone, Thomas. "Science, Art, and the Predispositions of Educational Researchers." *Educational Researcher* 30, no. 7 (2001), 24–28.

Belinda. Made a great Halloween costume for her son on the day we met.

Bernardez, Teresa. "Women and Anger: Cultural Prohibitions and the Feminine Ideal." *Work in Progress* 31, Wellesley, MA: Stone Centre Working Paper Series, 1988.

Bhabha, Homi. "Postcolonial Authority and Postmodern Guilt." In *Cultural Studies*, edited by Lawrence Grossberg, Cary Nelson, and Paula Treichler, 56–68. New York: Routledge, 1992.

———. *The Location of Culture*. London: Routledge, 1994.

Bold, Christine, Ric Knowles, and Belinda Leach. "Feminist Memorializing and Cultural Countermemory: The Case of Marianne's Park." *Signs* 28, no. 1 (2002), 125–48.

Brison, Susan. *Aftermath: Violence and the Remaking of a Self*. Princeton, NJ: Princeton University Press, 2002.

Britzman, Deborah, and Alice J. Pitt. "Speculation on Qualities of Difficult Knowledge in Teaching and Learning: An Experiment in Psychoanalytic Research." In *Doing Educational Research*, edited by Kenneth Tobin and Joe L. Kincheloe, 379–402. Boston, MA: Sense Publishers, 2006.

Brown, Laura. *Subversive Dialogues: Theory in Feminist Therapy*. New York: Basic Books, 1994.

Burman, Erica. "Fictioning Authority: Writing Experience in Feminist Teaching and Learning." *Psychodynamic Counselling* 7, no. 2 (2001), 1–19.

Burns, Leah. "Seriously. Are You Really an Artist? Humor and Integrity in a Community Mural Project." In *Wildfire: Art as Activism*, edited by Deborah Barndt, 25–36. Toronto: Sumach, 2006.

Butler, Judith. "Performative Acts and Gender Constitution: An Essay in Phenomenology and Feminist Theory." In *Performing Feminisms:*

Feminist Critical Theory and Theatre, edited by Sue Ellen Case, 270–82. Baltimore: John Hopkins University Press, 1990.

———. "Contingent Foundations: Feminism and the Question of 'Postmodernism.'" In *Feminists Theorize the Political*, edited by Judith Butler and Joan Scott, 3–21. New York: Routledge, 1992.

Cancian, Francesca M. "Participatory Research and Alternative Strategies for Activist Sociology." In *Feminism and Social Change: Bridging Theory and Practice*, edited by Heidi Gottfried, 187–205. Urbana, IL: University of Chicago Press, 1996.

Caruth, Cathy. "Introduction." In *Trauma: Explorations in Memory*, edited by Cathy Caruth, 3–12. Baltimore: John Hopkins University Press, 1995.

———, and Thomas Keenan. "The Aids Crisis Is Not Over: A Conversation with Gregg Bordowitz, Douglas Crimp and Laura Pinsky." In *Trauma: Explorations in Memory*, edited by Cathy Caruth, 256–72. Baltimore: John Hopkins University Press, 1995.

Castricano, Jodey. "Learning To Talk with Ghosts: Canadian Gothic and the Poetics of Haunting in Eden Robinson's *Monkey Beach*." *University of Toronto Quarterly* 75, no. 2 (2006), 801–13.

Cheryl. Is not intimidated by gadgets.

Christman, Jolley Bruce. "Working in the Field as a Female Friend." *Anthropology and Education Quarterly* 19, no. 2 (1988), 70–85.

Code, Lorraine. "How Do We Know? Questions of Method in Feminist Practice." In *Changing Methods: Feminists Transforming Practice*, edited by Sandra Burt and Lorraine Code, 13–44. Peterborough, ON: Broadview, 1995.

Conquergood, Dwight. "Performing as a Moral Act: Ethical Dimensions of the Ethnography of Performance." In *Turning Points in Qualitative Research: Tying Knots in a Handkerchief*, edited by Norman K. Denzin and Yvonna S. Lincoln, 397–414. Walnut Creek, CA: AltaMira, 2003.

———. "Rethinking Ethnography: Towards a Critical Cultural Politics." In *Turning Points in Qualitative Research: Tying Knots in a Handkerchief*, edited by Norman K. Denzin and Yvonna S. Lincoln, 351–74. Walnut Creek, CA: AltaMira, 2003.

Cotterill, Pamela. "Interviewing Women: Issues of Friendship, Vulnerability, and Power." *Women's Studies International Forum* 15, no. 5/6 (1992), 593–606.

Cricket. Steals your socks but only chews her own toys.

Crowe, Roewan. "Crafting Tales of Trauma: Will This Winged Monster Fly?" In *Provoked By Art: Theorizing Arts—Informed Research*, edited by Ardra Cole, Lorri Neilsen, J. Gary Knowles, and Teresa C. Luciani, 123–33. Halifax, NS: Backalong Books, 2004.

D'Aponte, Mimi Gisolfi. "Native Women Playwrights: Transmitters, Healers, Transformers." *Journal of Dramatic Theory and Criticism* 14 (1999), 99–108.

David. His life isn't actually meaningless (I think).

Davis, Liane V., and Meera Srinivasan. "Listening to the Voices of Battered Women: What Helps Them Escape Violence." *Affilia: Journal of Women and Social Work* 10 (1995), 49–69.

Dawn. Is an amazing decorator.

de Freitas, Liz. "Reclaiming Rigour as Trust: The Playful Process of Writing Fiction." In *Provoked by Art: Theorizing Arts-Informed Research*, edited by Ardra Cole, Lorri Neilsen, J. Gary Knowles, and Teresa C. Luciani, 262–72. Halifax, NS: Backalong Books, 2004.

Denzin, Norman K. "Presidential Address on *the Sociological Imagination* Revisited." *Sociological Quarterly* 31, no. 1 (1990), 1–22.

Derrida, Jacques. *Of Grammatology.* Translated by Gayatri Chakravorty Spivak. Baltimore: John Hopkins University Press, 1976.

———. *Spectres of Marx: The State of the Debt, the Work of Mourning, and the New International.* Translated by Peggy Kamuf. New York: Routledge, 1994.

———. *Archive Fever: A Freudian Impression.* Chicago: University of Illinois Press, 1996.

DeVault, Marjorie L. *Liberating Method: Feminism and Social Research.* Philadephia: Temple University Press, 1999.

———, and Glenda Gross. "Feminist Interviewing: Experience, Talk and Knowledge." In *Handbook of Feminist Research: Theory and Praxis*, edited by Sharlene Nagy Hesse-Biber, 173–98. Thousand Oaks, CA: Sage, 2006.

Didion, Joan. *The Year of Magical Thinking.* New York: Knopf, 2005.

Dora. Was a cat named Whiskers from ages 2–4.

Cast

Dr. White. Goes snowboarding when stuff starts getting her down.

Dunlop, Rishma. "Scar Tissue, Testimony, Beauty: Notebooks on Theory." In *Provoked By Art: Theorizing Arts-Informed Research*, edited by Ardra Cole, Lorri Neilsen, J. Gary Knowles, and Teresa C. Luciani, 84–99. Halifax, NS: Backalong Books, 2004.

Edkins, Jenny. *Trauma and the Memory of Politics*. Cambridge, UK: Cambridge University Press, 2003.

Eisner, E.W. "The Promise and Perils of Alternative Forms of Data Representation." *Educational Researcher* 26, no. 6 (1997), 4–20.

Ellis, Carolyn. "Being Real: Moving Inward Toward Social Change." *Qualitative Studies in Education* 15, no. 4 (2002), 399–406.

Eppert, Claudia. "Relearning Questions: Responding to the Ethical Address of Past and Present Others." In *Between Hope and Despair: Pedagogy and the Remembrance of Historical Trauma*, edited by Roger Simon, Sharon Rosenburg, and Claudia Eppert, 213–30. Oxford: Rowman & Littlefield, 2000.

Erikson, Kai. "Notes on Trauma and Community." In *Trauma: Explorations in Memory*, edited by Cathy Caruth, 182–99. Baltimore: John Hopkins University Press, 1995.

Felman, Shoshana. "Education and Crisis, or the Vicissitudes of Teaching." In *Trauma: Explorations in Memory*, edited by Cathy Caruth, 13–60. Baltimore: John Hopkins University Press, 1995.

Finley, Susan, and Gary J. Knowles. "Researcher as Artist/Artist as Researcher." *Qualitative Inquiry* 1, no. 1 (1995), 110–42.

Flax, Jane. "The End of Innocence." In *Feminists Theorize the Political*, edited by Judith Butler and Joan Scott, 445–63. New York: Routledge, 1992.

Flemons, Douglas, and Shelley Green. "Stories that Conform/Stories that Transform: A Conversation in Four Parts." In *Ethnographically Speaking: Autoethnography, Literature, and Aesthetics*, edited by Carolyn Ellis and Arthur P. Bochner, 87–94; 115–21; 165–69; 187–90. Walnut Creek, CA: AltaMira, 2002.

Flood, Robert Louis. "The Relationship of 'Systems Thinking' to Action Research." In *Handbook of Action Research*, edited by Peter Reason and Hilary Bradbury, 133–44. Thousand Oaks, CA:

Sage, 2006.

Foley, Douglas. "Critical Ethnography: The Reflexive Turn." *Qualitative Studies in Education* 15, no. 5 (2002), 490–96.

Frank, Arthur W. "Between the Story and the Ride: Illness and Remoralization." In *Ethnographically Speaking: Autoethnography, Literature, and Aesthetics*, edited by Carolyn Ellis and Arthur P Bochner, 357–71. Walnut Creek, CA: AltaMira, 2002.

Freud, Sigmund. "Mourning and Melancholia." In *Collected Papers, Vol. 4*, edited by Ernest Jones, 152–70. New York: Basic Books, 1917/1959.

Fulford, Robert. *The Triumph of Narrative: Storytelling in the Age of Mass Culture*. Toronto, ON: Anansi, 1999.

Garamone, Pariss. "Tellingsmiths: The Work of Planting Trees, the Politics of Memory." In *Wildfire: Art as Activism*, edited by Deborah Barndt, 160–73. Toronto: Sumach, 2006.

Gergen, Kenneth J., and Mary M. Gergen. "Ethnographic Representation as Relationship." In *Ethnographically Speaking: Autoethnography, Literature, and Aesthetics*, edited by Carolyn Ellis and Arthur P. Bochner, 11–34. Walnut Creek, CA: AltaMira, 2002.

Gilfus, Mary E., et al. "Research on Violence Against Women: Creating Survivor-Informed Collaborations." *Violence Against Women* 15 (1999), 1194–1212.

Gillies, Val, and Pam Alldred. "The Ethics of Intention: Research as a Political Tool." In *Ethics in Qualitative Research*, edited by Melanie Mauthner, Maxine Birch, Julie Jessop, and Tina Miller, 33–52. London: Sage, 2002.

Gillis, J. Roy, and Shaindl Diamond. "Same-Sex Partner Abuse: Challenges to the Existing Paradigms of Intimate Violence Theory." In *Cruel But Not Unusual: Violence in the Canadian Family*, edited by Ramona Allagia and Cathy Vine, 127–46. Waterloo, ON: Wilfrid Laurier University Press, 2006.

Glesne, Corinne. "That Rare Feeling: Re-presenting Research Through Poetic Transcription." *Qualitative Inquiry* 3, no. 2 (1997), 202–21.

Goldman, Marlene. "A Dangerous Circuit: Loss and the Boundaries of Racialized Subjectivity in Joy Kogawa's *Obasan* and Kerri Sakamoto's *The Electrical Field*." *Modern Fiction Studies* 48, no.

2 (2002), 362–88.

———. and Joanne Saul. "Talking With Ghosts: Haunting in Canadian Cultural Production." *University of Toronto Quarterly* 75, no. 2 (2006), 645–55.

Goodall, H.L. *Writing Qualitative Inquiry: Self, Stories and Academic Life*. Walnut Creek, CA: Left Coast, 2008.

Gordon, Avery. *Ghostly Matters: Haunting and the Sociological Imagination*. 2nd ed. Minneapolis: University of Minnesota Press, 2008.

Gorelick, Sherry. "Contradictions of Feminist Methodology." In *Feminism and Social Change: Bridging Theory and Practice*, edited by Heidi Gottfried, 23–45. Urbana, IL: University of Chicago Press, 1996.

Gottschalk, Simon. "Postmodern Sensibilities and Ethnographic Possibilities." In *Fiction and Social Research: By Ice Or Fire*, edited by Anna Banks and Stephen P. Banks, 205–34. Walnut Creek, CA: AltaMira, 1998.

Graham, Erin. "This Trauma is Not Vicarious." *Canadian Woman Studies* 25, no. 1–2 (2006), 17–23.

Greenblatt, Stephen. *Marvelous Possessions: The Wonder of the New World*. Chicago: University of Chicago Press, 1992.

Gubar, Susan. "Empathic Identification in Anne Michael's *Fugitive Pieces:* Masculinity and Poetry After Auschwitz." *Signs* 28, no. 1 (2002), 249–75.

Hall, Stuart. "Encoding/Decoding." In *Media and Cultural Studies: Key Works*, edited by Meenakshi Gigi Durham and Douglas M. Kellner, 163–173. London: Blackwell, 1980.

Halse, Christine, and Anne Honey. "Unraveling Ethics: Illuminating the Moral Dilemmas of Research Ethics." *Signs: Journal of Women in Culture and Society* 30, no. 4 (2005), 2141–62.

Hantzis, Darlene. "Reflections on 'A Dialogue With Friends': 'Performing' the 'Other/Self' OJA 1995." In *The Future of Performance Studies: Visions and Revisions,* edited by Sheron J. Dailey, 14–22. Annadale, VA: NCA, 1998.

Haraway, Donna. "Situated Knowledges: The Science Question in Feminism and the Privilege of Partial Perspective." In *Turning Points in Qualitative Research: Tying Knots in a Handkerchief,* edited by Norman K. Denzin and Yvonna S. Lincoln, 21–46.

Walnut Creek, CA: AltaMira, 2003.

Harding, Sandra, and Kathryn Norberg. "New Feminist Approaches to Social Science Methodologies: An Introduction." *Signs: Journal of Women in Culture and Society* 30, no. 4 (2005), 2009–15.

Harvey, Mary R., Elliot G. Mishler, Karestan Koenen, and Patricia A. Harney. "In the Aftermath of Sexual Abuse: Making and Remaking Meaning in Narratives of Trauma and Recovery." *Narrative Inquiry* 10, no. 2 (2001), 291–311.

Haugo, Ann. "Negotiating Hybridity: Native Women's Performance as Cultural Persistence." *Women and Performance* 7, no. 14–15 (1995), 125–41.

Heather. Wears a funky hat.

Henderson, Angela D. "Preparing Feminist Facilitators: Assisting Abused Women in Transitional or Support-Group Settings." *Journal of Psychosocial Nursing & Mental Health Services* 36, no. 3 (1998), 25–33.

Herman, Judith. *Trauma and Recovery.* New York: Basic Books, 1997.

Heron, John, and Peter Reason. "The Practice of Co-Operative Inquiry: Research 'With' Rather Than 'On' People." In *Handbook of Action Research*, edited by Peter Reason and Hilary Bradbury, 179–88. Thousand Oaks, CA: Sage, 2006.

Hill Collins, Patricia. "Learning From the Outsider Within: The Sociological Significance of Black Feminist Thought." In *Beyond Methodology*, edited by Mary Margaret Fonow and Judith A Cook, 35–59. Bloomington: Indiana University Press, 1991.

———. "Toward a New Vision: Race, Class and Gender as Categories of Analysis and Connection." In *Women's Voices, Feminist Visions*, edited by Susan Shaw, 72–80. Mountain View, CA: Mayfield Publishing, 2001.

Hippensteele, Susan K. "Activist Research and Social Narratives: Dialectics of Power, Privilege, and Institutional Change." In *Researching Sexual Violence Against Women: Methodological and Personal Perspectives*, edited by Martin D. Schwartz, 86–100. Thousand Oaks, CA: Sage, 1997.

Hodgins, Peter. "Our Haunted Present: Cultural Memory in Question." *Topia: Canadian Journal of Cultural Studies* 12 (2004), 99–108.

hooks, bell. *Talking Back: Thinking Feminist, Thinking Black.* Boston:

South End, 1989.

Horsman, Jenny. "Literacy Learning for Survivors of Trauma: Acting 'Normal.'" In *Violence Against Women: New Canadian Perspectives*, edited by Katherine M.J. McKenna and June Larkin, 263–72. Toronto: Innana Publishing, 2002.

Jen.   Can make a cup of coffee last a long, long time.

June.   Likes ballroom dancing.

Kauffman, Linda S. "The Long Goodbye: Against Personal Testimony, Or an Infant Grifter Grows Up." In *American Feminist Thought at Century's End: A Reader*, edited by Linda S. Kauffman, 258–77. Cambridge, MA: Blackwell, 1993.

Kearney, Margaret H. "Enduring Love: A Grounded Formal Theory of Women's Experience of Domestic Violence." *Research in Nursing and Health* 24 (2001), 270–82.

Kelly, Liz, Sheila Burton, and Linda Regan. "Researching Women's Lives or Studying Women's Oppression? Reflections on What Constitutes Feminist Research." In *Researching Women's Lives from a Feminist Perspective*, edited by Mary Maynard and June Purvis, 27–48. London: Taylor & Francis, 1994.

Kelly, Patty. "Trauma Narratives in Canadian Fiction: A Chronotopic Analysis of Anne Michael's *Fugitive Pieces*." Paper presented at the Making Sense of Health, Illness and Disease, Oxford, 2006.

Kendrick, Karen. "Producing the Battered Woman." In *Community Activism and Feminist Politics: Organizing Across Race, Class and Gender*, edited by Nancy Naples, 151–174. New York: Routledge, 1998.

Kesby, Mike. "Retheorizing Empowerment-Through-Participation as a Performance in Space: Beyond Tyranny to Transformation." *Signs: Journal of Women in Culture and Society* 30, no. 4 (2005), 2037–65.

Krystal, Henry. "Trauma and Aging: A Thirty Year Follow-Up." In *Trauma: Explorations in Memory*, edited by Cathy Caruth, 76–99. Baltimore: John Hopkins University Press, 1995.

LaCapra, Dominic. "Trauma, Absence, Loss." *Critical Inquiry* 25, no. 4

(1999): 696–727.

Lal, Jayati. "Situating Locations: The Politics of Self, Identity, and 'Other' in Living and Writing the Text." In *Feminist Dilemmas in Fieldwork*, edited by Diane L. Wolf, 185–214. Boulder, CO: Westview, 1996.

Landenburger, Karen. "The Dynamics of Leaving and Recovering from an Abusive Relationship." *Journal of Obstetric, Gynaecologic, and Neonatal Nursing* 27, no. 6 (1998), 700–06.

Langellier, Kristin M. "Personal Narrative, Performance, Performativity: Two or Three Things I Know for Sure." In *Turning Points in Qualitative Research: Tying Knots in a Handkerchief*, edited by Norman K. Denzin and Yvonna S. Lincoln, 441–68. Walnut Creek, CA: AltaMira, 2003.

Lash, Heather. "You Are My Sunshine: Refugee Participation in Performance." In *Wildfire: Art as Activism*, edited by Deborah Barndt, 221–29. Toronto: Sumach, 2006.

Lather, Patti. "Research as Praxis." *Harvard Educational Review* 56, no. 3 (1986): 257–77.

———, and Chris Smithies. *Troubling the Angels: Women Living with HIV/AIDS*. Boulder, CO: Westview, 1997.

———. *Getting Lost: Feminist Efforts toward a Double(d) Science*. Albany: State University of New York, 2007.

Laub, Dori. "Truth and Testimony: The Process and the Struggle." In *Trauma: Explorations in Memory*, edited by Cathy Caruth, 61–75. Baltimore: John Hopkins University Press, 1995.

Law, John. *After Method: Mess in Social Science Research*. New York: Routledge, 2004.

Levy, Sophie. "'This Dark Echo Calls Him Home': Writing Father-Daughter Incest Narratives in Canadian Immigrant Fiction." *University of Toronto Quarterly* 71, no. 4 (2002), 864–80.

Lincoln, Yvonna S. "Engaging Sympathies: Relationships between Action Research and Social Constructivism." In *Handbook of Action Research*, edited by Peter Reason and Hilary Bradbury, 124–32. Thousand Oaks, CA: Sage, 2006.

Lykes, M. Brinton, and Erzulie Coquillon. "Participatory and Action Research and Feminisms." In *Handbook of Feminist Research: Theory and Praxis*, edited by Sharlene Nagy Hesse-Biber,

297–326. Thousand Oaks, CA: Sage, 2006.

Lyons, Lenore, and Janine Chipperfield. "(De)Constructing the Interview: A Critique of the Participatory Model." *Resources for Feminist Research* 28, no. 1/2 (2000), 33–48.

Maclure, Molly. "Telling Transitions: Boundary Work in Narratives of Becoming an Action Researcher." *British Educational Research Journal* 22, no. 3 (1996), 273–86.

Maguire, Patricia. *Doing Participatory Research: A Feminist Approach.* Amherst, MA: The Centre for International Education, 1987.

Mamet, David. *Three Uses of the Knife: On the Nature and Purpose of Drama.* New York: Vintage, 1998.

Mann, Ruth M. *Who Owns Domestic Abuse? The Local Politics of a Social Problem.* Toronto: University of Toronto Press, 2000.

Margo. Teaches fly-fishing.

Markussen, Turid. "Practicing Performativity: Transformative Moments in Research." *European Journal of Women's Studies* 12, no. 3 (2005), 329–44.

Mars, Tanya, and Johanna Householder. *Caught in the Act: An Anthology of Performance Art By Canadian Women.* Toronto: YYZ Books, 2004.

Martz, Diane J. Forsdick, and Deborah Bryson Saraurer. "Domestic Violence and the Experiences of Rural Women in East Central Saskatchewan." In *Violence Against Women: New Canadian Perspectives,* edited by Katherine M.J. McKenna and June Larkin, 163–95. Toronto: Innana Publications, 2002.

Mason, Jody. "Searching for the Doorway: Dionne Brandt's *Thirsty.*" *University of Toronto Quarterly* 75, no. 2 (2006), 784–800.

Mauthner, Melanie, and Andrea Doucet. "Reflections on a Voice-Centered Relational Method." In *Feminist Dilemmas in Qualitative Research: Public Knowledge and Private Lives,* edited by Jane Ribbens and Rosalind Edwards, 119–46. London: Sage, 1998.

McDonald, Susan. "Asking Questions and Asking More: Reflections on Feminist Participatory Research." *Resources for Feminist Research* 30, no. 1–2 (2003), 77–100.

McIntyre, Maura. "Ethic and Aesthetics: The Goodness of Arts-Informed Research." In *Provoked by Art: Theorizing Arts-Informed Research,* edited by Ardra Cole, Lorri Neilsen, J. Gary Knowles, and Teresa

C. Luciani, 251–61. Halifax, NS: Backalong Books, 2004.

McRobbie, Angela. "The Politics of Feminist Research: Between Talk, Text and Action." *Feminist Review* 12 (1982), 46–57.

Metasophie. An adjacent voice, critical of my theory, methods, form, and function, grounded in the body and emotion, and full of wants.

Michaels, Anne. *The Winter Vault.* Toronto: McClelland & Stewart, 2009.

Mienczakowski, Jim. "The Theatre of Ethnography: The Reconstruction of Ethnography into Theatre with Emancipatory Potential." In *Turning Points in Qualitative Research: Tying Knots in a Handkerchief,* edited by Norman K. Denzin and Yvonna S. Lincoln, 415–32. Walnut Creek, CA: AltaMira, 2003.

Miller, Jean Baker, and Irene Pierce Stiver. *The Healing Connection: How Women Form Relationships in Therapy and Life.* Boston: Beacon Press, 1997.

Mohanty, Chandra Talpade. "Sisterhood, Coalition, and the Politics of Experience." In *Feminism Without Borders: Decolonizing Theory,* edited by Chandra T. Mohanty, 106–23. Durham, NC: Duke University Press, 2003.

Molly. Has tiny feet and was very kind to me.

Naples, Nancy. *Feminism and Method: Ethnography, Discourse Analysis, and Activist Research.* New York: Routledge, 2003.

———, and Emily Clark. "Feminist Participatory Research and Empowerment: Going Public as Survivors of Childhood Sexual Abuse." In *Feminism and Social Change: Bridging Theory and Practice,* edited by Heidi Gottfried, 160–86. Urbana, IL: University of Chicago Press, 1996.

Noddings, Nel. *Caring: A Feminine Approach to Ethics and Moral Education.* Berkeley: University of California Press, 1984.

Novak, Amy. "Textual Hauntings: Narrating History, Memory, and Silence in *The English Patient*." *Studies in the Novel* 36, no. 2 (2004), 206–31.

Oakley, Anne. "Gender, Methodology and People's Ways of Knowing: Some Problems with Feminism and the Paradigm Debate in Social

Science." *Sociology* 32, no. 4 (1998), 707–32.

Olive. Had her home bombed out twice during the war.

O'Neill, Edward. "Traumatic Postmodern Histories: Velvet Goldmine's Phantasmic Testimonies." *Camera Obscura* 19, no. 3 (2004), 157–85.

Orlie, Melissa. *Living Ethically, Acting Politically.* Ithaca, NY: Cornell University Press, 1997.

Patocka, Jan. *Heretical Essays in the Philosophy of History.* Translated by Erazim Kohak. Edited by James Dodd. Chicago: Open Court, 1996.

Patraka, Vivian M. "Feminism and the Jewish Subject in the Plays of Sachs, Atlan, and Schenkar." In *Performing Feminisms: Feminist Critical Theory and Theatre*, edited by Sue Ellen Case, 160–74. Baltimore: John Hopkins University Press, 1990.

Pelias, Ronald J. *A Methodology of the Heart: Evoking Academic and Daily Life.* Walnut Creek, CA: AltaMira, 2004.

Phelan, Peggy. "Reciting the Citation of Others; Or, a Second Introduction." In *Acting Out: Feminist Performances*, edited by Lynda Hart and Peggy Phelan, 13–34. Ann Arbor: University of Michigan Press, 1993.

Pick, Zuzana. "Storytelling and Resistance: The Documentary Practice of Alanis Obomsawin." In *Gendering the Nation: Canadian Women's Cinema*, edited by Kay Armatage, Kass Banning, Brenda Longfellow, and Janine Marchessault, 76–93. Toronto: University of Toronto Press, 1999.

Piirto, Jane. "The Question of Quality and Qualifications: Writing Inferior Poems as Qualitative Research." *Qualitative Studies in Education* 15, no. 4 (2002), 431–45.

Pink, Sarah. *Doing Visual Ethnography: Images, Media and Representation in Research.* Thousand Oaks, CA: Sage, 2001.

Potts, Karen, and Leslie Brown. "Becoming an Anti-Oppressive Researcher." In *Research as Resistance: Critical Indigenous and Anti-Oppressive Approaches*, edited by Leslie Brown and Susan Strega, 255–86. Toronto: Canadian Scholars', 2003.

Prendergast, Monica. "Poem Is What? Poetic Inquiry in Qualitative

Social Science Research." *International Review of Qualitative Research* 1, no. 4 (2009), 541–68.

Prentki, Tim, and Jan Selman. *Popular Theatre in Political Culture: Britain and Canada in Focus*. Bristol, UK: Intellect Books, 2000.

Presser, Lois. "Negotiating Power and Narrative in Research: Implications for Feminist Methodology." *Signs: Journal of Women in Culture and Society* 30, no. 4 (2005), 2067–90.

Price, Lisa S. *Feminist Frameworks: Building Theory on Violence Against Women*. Black Point, NS: Fernwood Publishing, 2005.

Ranck, Jody. "Beyond Reconciliation: Memory and Alterity in Post-Genocide Rwanda." In *Between Hope and Despair: Pedagogy and the Remembrance of Historical Trauma*, edited by Roger Simon, Sharon Rosenburg, and Claudia Eppert, 187–212. Oxford: Rowman & Littlefield, 2000.

Randall, Margaret. *When I Look Into the Mirror and See You: Women, Terror and Resistance*. New Brunswick, NJ: Rutgers University Press, 2003.

Razack, Sherene. "Storytelling for Social Change." *Gender and Education* 5, no. 1 (1993), 55–70.

Read, Robyn. "Witnessing the Workshop Process of Judith Thompson's *Capture Me*." In *The Masks of Judith Thompson*, edited by Ric Knowles, 118–25. Toronto: Playwrights Canada Press, 2006.

Reason, Peter, and Hilary Bradbury. "Introduction: Inquiry and Participation in Search of a World Worthy of Human Aspiration." In *Handbook of Action Research*, edited by Peter Reason and Hilary Bradbury, 1–14. Thousand Oaks, CA: Sage, 2006.

Richardson, Laurel. *Fields of Play*. New Brunswick, NJ: Rutgers University Press, 1997.

———. "Reading for Another: A Method for Addressing Some Feminist Research Dilemmas." In *Handbook of Feminist Research: Theory and Praxis*, edited by Sharlene Nagy Hesse-Biber, 459–67. Thousand Oaks, CA: Sage, 2006.

Ristock, Janice. *No More Secrets: Violence in Lesbian Relationships*. London: Routledge, 2002.

Rowan, John. "The Humanistic Approach to Action Research." In *Handbook of Action Research*, edited by Peter Reason and Hilary

Bradbury, 114–23. Thousand Oaks, CA: Sage, 2006.

Ruth. Likes deep talks long past tuck-in.

Salverson, Julie. "Anxiety and Contact in Attending to a Play about Land Mines." In *Between Hope and Despair: Pedagogy and the Remembrance of Historical Trauma,* edited by Roger Simon, Sharon Rosenburg, and Claudia Eppert, 59–74. Oxford, UK: Rowman & Littlefield, 2000.

Sarah. Is smart, generous, insightful, funny, and supportive. She gives me hope.

Schechner, Richard. *Between Theatre and Anthropology.* Philadelphia: University of Pennsylvania Press, 1985.

Shawn. Occasionally performs routine tasks (including shaving) with his eyes closed just in case someday he goes blind.

Shepard, Benjamin. "Play, Creativity and the New Community Organizing." *Journal of Progressive Human Services* 16, no. 2 (2005), 47–69.

Shirley. Loves her garden.

Silverman, Kaja. *The Threshold of the Visible World.* New York: Routledge, 1996.

Simon, Roger. "The Paradoxical Practice of Zakhor." In *Between Hope and Despair: Pedagogy and the Remembrance of Historical Trauma,* edited by Roger Simon, Sharon Rosenburg, and Claudia Eppert, 9–25. Oxford: Rowman & Littlefield, 2000.

———. Sharon Rosenburg, and Claudia Eppert. "Introduction: Between Hope and Despair: The Pedagogical Encounter of Historical Remembrance." In *Between Hope and Despair: Pedagogy and the Remembrance of Historical Trauma,* edited by Roger Simon, Sharon Rosenburg, and Claudia Eppert, 1–8. Oxford: Rowman & Littlefield, 2000.

Skeggs, Beverley. "Situating the Production of Feminist Ethnography." In *Researching Women's Lives From a Feminist Perspective,* edited by Mary Maynard and June Purvis, 72–92. London: Taylor & Francis, 1994.

Smith, Linda Tuhiwai. *Decolonizing Methodologies.* London: Zed Books, 1999.

Smith, Marilyn. "Recovery from Intimate Partner Violence: A Difficult

Journey." *Issues in Mental Health Nursing* 24 (2003), 543–73.

Sophie. Would like to thank the academy.

Stacey, Judith. "Can There Be a Feminist Ethnography?" *Women's Studies International Forum* 11, no. 1 (1998), 21–27.

Stella. Has well groomed fingernails.

Sugiman, Pamela. "Memories of Internment: Narrating Japanese Women's Life Stories." *Canadian Journal of Sociology* 29, no. 3 (2004), 359–88.

Sullivan, Graeme. *Art Practice as Research: Inquiry in the Visual Arts.* Thousand Oaks, CA: Sage, 2005.

Swift, Carolyn F. "Women and Violence: Breaking the Connection." *Work in Progress* 27. Wellesley, MA: Stone Centre Working Paper Series, 1987.

Tahirih. Bumps into lots of things.

Tammy. Has gone back to school.

Thompson, Judith. *The Crackwalker.* Toronto: Playwrights Canada Press, 1980.

———. *Perfect Pie.* Toronto: Playwrights Canada Press, 1999.

Todd, Sarah, and Colleen Lundy. "Framing Woman Abuse: A Structural Perspective." In *Cruel But Not Unusual: Violence in Canadian Families,* edited by Ramona Allagia and Cathy Vine, 327–69. Waterloo, ON: Wilfrid Laurier University Press, 2006.

Todorov, Tzvetan. "A Dialogic Criticism?" *Raritan* 4 (1984), 64–76.

Trinh, T. Minh-ha. *Woman, Native, Other: Writing Postcoloniality and Feminism.* Bloomington: Indiana University Press, 1989.

Tschofen, Monique. "Repetition, Compulsion and Representation in Atom Egoyan's Films." In *North of Everything: English-Canadian Cinema Since 1980,* edited by William Beard and Jerry White, 166–83. Edmonton, AB: University of Alberta Press, 2002.

Tutty, Leslie M. "Identifying, Assessing, and Treating Male Perpetrators and Abused Women." In *Cruel But Not Unusual: Violence in Canadian Families,* edited by Ramona Allagia and Cathy Vine, 371–96. Waterloo, ON: Wilfrid Laurier University Press, 2006.

Ubah. Is allergic to cats.

Ubersophie. An over-Sophie, similar to Augusto Boal's cop-in-the-head, full of shoulds.

van der Kolk, Bessel A., and Onno van der Hart. "The Intrusive Past: The Flexibility of Memory and the Engraving of Trauma." In *Trauma: Explorations in Memory*, edited by Cathy Caruth, 158–82. Baltimore: John Hopkins University Press, 1995.

Victoria. Has a great laugh.

Visweswaran, Kamala. *Fictions of Feminist Ethnography*. Minneapolis: University of Minnesota Press, 1994.

Vizenor, Gerald. "A Postmodern Introduction." In *Narrative Chance*, edited by Gerald Vizenor, 3–16. Albuquerque: University of New Mexico Press, 1989.

———. "Aesthetics of Survivance: Literary Theory and Practice." In *Survivance: Narratives of Native Presence*, edited by Gerald Vizenor, 1-24. Lincoln, NE: University of Nebraska Press, 2008.

Wachtel, Eleanor. "An Interview with Judith Thompson." In *The Masks of Judith Thompson*, edited by Ric Knowles, 43–49. Toronto: Playwrights Canada Press, 2006.

Walcott, Rinaldo. "'It's My Nature': The Discourse and Experience of Black Canadian Music." In *Slippery Pastimes: Reading the Popular in Canadian Culture*, edited by Joan Nicks and Jeannette Sloniowski, 263–78. Waterloo, ON: Wilfrid Laurier University Press, 2002.

Wark, Jane. "Dressed to Thrill: Costume, Body and Dress in Canadian Performance Art." In *Caught in the Act: An Anthology of Performance Art by Canadian Women*, edited by Tanya Mars and Johanna Householder, 86–101. Toronto: YYZ Books, 2004.

Wiesel, Elie. "The Holocaust as Literary Inspiration." In *Dimensions of the Holocaust*, edited by Elliot Lefkovitz, 5–19. Evanston, IL: Northwestern University Press, 1990.

Williams, Kimberle Crenshaw. "Mapping the Margins: Intersectionality, Identity Politics, and Violence Against Women of Color." *Stanford Law Review* 43, no. 6 (1991), 1241–99.

Wolf, Diane L. "Situating Feminist Dilemmas in Fieldwork." In *Feminist Dilemmas in Fieldwork*, edited by Diane L. Wolf, 1–55. Boulder, CO: Westview, 1996.

Wuest, Judith, and Marilyn Merritt-Gray. "Not Going Back: Sustaining the Separation in the Process of Leaving Abusive Relationships." *Violence Against Women* 5, no. 2 (1999), 110–33.

Wylie, Herb. "It Takes More Than Mortality To Make Somebody Dead: Spectres of History in Margaret Sweatman's *When Alice Lay Down With Peter.*" *University of Toronto Quarterly* 75, no. 2 (2006), 735–51.

You, the Reader *(fill in the blank)* _____.

Young, Alannah Earl, and Denise Nadeau. "Decolonising the Body: Restoring Sacred Vitality." *Atlantis* 29, no. 2 (2005), 13–22.

Zamora, Lois Parkinson, and Wendy B. Faris. "Introduction: Daiquiri Birds and Flaubertian Parrot(ie)s." In *Magical Realism: Theory, History, Community*, edited by Lois Parkinson Zamora and Wendy B. Faris, 1–14. Durham, NC: Duke University Press, 1995.

INDEX

ABOUT THE AUTHOR

Sophie Tamas is a postdoctoral fellow in Emotional Geography at Queen's University in Kingston, Canada, and an award-winning playwright. Her current research examines sites of memory work, where we make sense and use of loss. She has a PhD and MA in Canadian Studies from Carleton University (Ottawa, Canada). Her publications focus on the ethical and methodological challenges of producing knowledge in sites of trauma. Her dissertation, an earlier version of this manuscript, was short-listed for the AERA Arts-Based Dissertation Award and won the 2011 Outstanding Dissertation Award from the International Institute for Qualitative Methodology. She lives in small-town Ontario with her partner, three teenage daughters, two dogs, two cats, and a fish.

green press
INITIATIVE

Left Coast Press is committed to preserving ancient forests and natural resources. We elected to print this title on 30% post consumer recycled paper, processed chlorine free. As a result, for this printing, we have saved:

2 Trees (40' tall and 6-8" diameter)
1 Million BTUs of Total Energy
184 Pounds of Greenhouse Gases
831 Gallons of Wastewater
53 Pounds of Solid Waste

Left Coast Press made this paper choice because our printer, Thomson-Shore, Inc., is a member of Green Press Initiative, a nonprofit program dedicated to supporting authors, publishers, and suppliers in their efforts to reduce their use of fiber obtained from endangered forests.

For more information, visit www.greenpressinitiative.org

Environmental impact estimates were made using the Environmental Defense Paper Calculator. For more information visit: www.papercalculator.org.